UNITED STATES AIR FORCE
STATISTICAL DIGEST
1948

THIRD ANNUAL EDITION

PREPARED BY
STATISTICAL SERVICES
COMPTROLLER, HQ U S AIR FORCE
WASHINGTON, DC

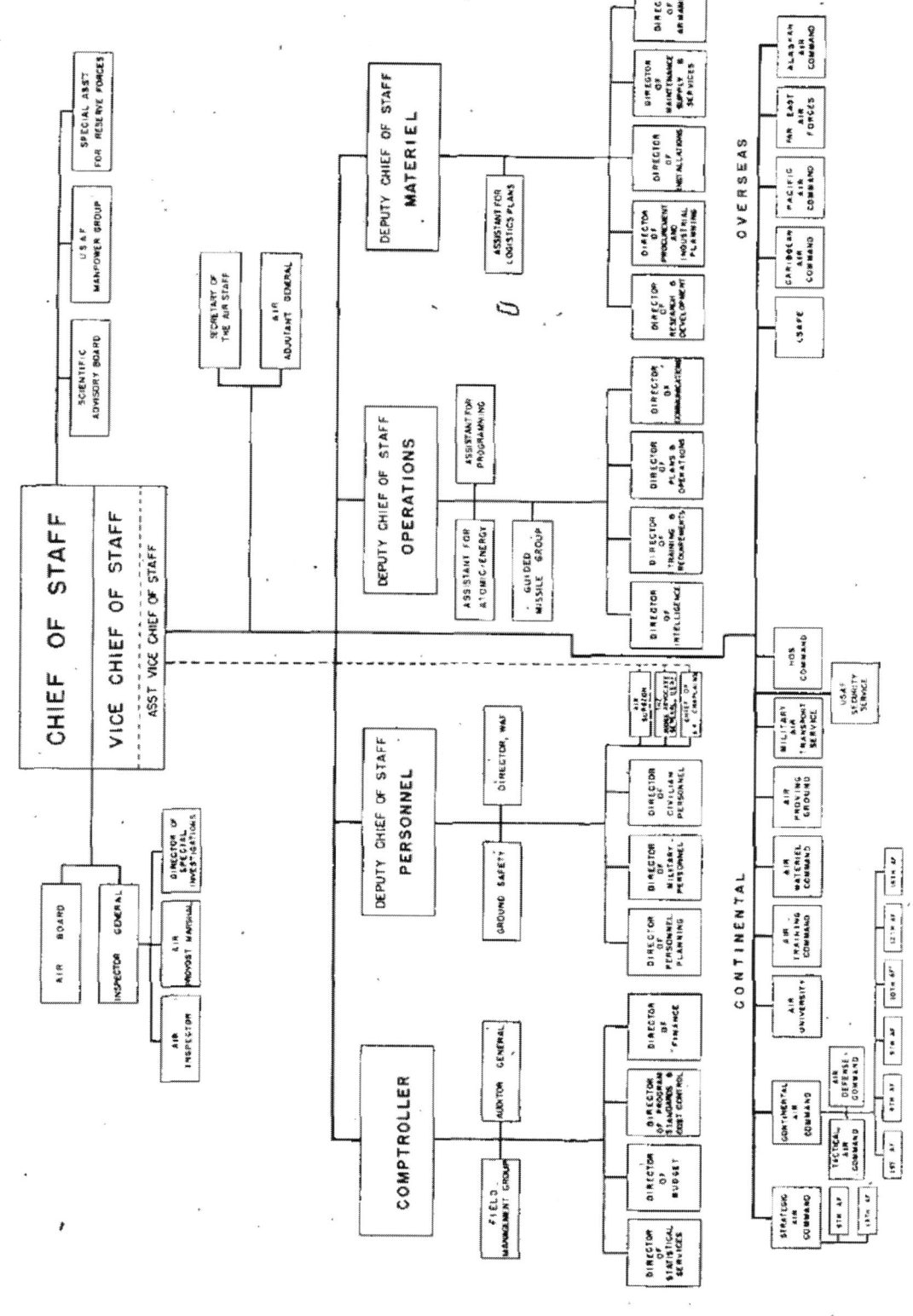

*AFR 5-24
1-2

AIR FORCE REGULATION)
NO. 5-24)

DEPARTMENT OF THE AIR FORCE
WASHINGTON, 20 SEPTEMBER 1948

PUBLICATIONS

United States Air Force Statistical Digest

	Paragraph
Official Statistical Yearbook	1
Distribution	2

1. **Official Statistical Yearbook.** The "United States Air Force Statistical Digest" prepared, published, and distributed by Headquarters USAF (Directorate of Statistical Services, Office of Comptroller) is hereby designated as the official Air Force statistical yearbook for the presentation of summary statistics on all phases of Air Force activity, strength, and operations.

2. **Distribution.** A limited distribution of this digest will be made as determined by Headquarters USAF.

BY ORDER OF THE SECRETARY OF THE AIR FORCE:

HOYT S. VANDENBERG
Chief of Staff, United States Air Force

OFFICIAL:

L. L. JUDGE
Colonel, USAF
Air Adjutant General

DISTRIBUTION:
B

------

*This Regulation supersedes AFL 5-3, 28 April 1947.

CONTENTS

FOREWORD		VII
GLOSSARY		VIII

PART I - TACTICAL UNITS

INTRODUCTION 1

Section I - *Number of Tactical Groups and Squadrons*

Table 1 - Tactical Groups and Separate Squadrons, By Type, in Continental US and Overseas, By Month: Jan through Dec, 1948 2

Table 2 - Tactical Groups and Separate Squadrons, By Type, US Air Forces in Europe By Month: Jan through Dec, 1948 5

Table 3 - Tactical Groups and Separate Squadrons, By Type, Caribbean Air Command, By Month: Jan through Dec, 1948 6

Table 4 - Tactical Groups and Separate Squadrons, By Type, Alaskan Air Command, By Month: Jan through Dec, 1948 7

Table 5 - Tactical Groups and Separate Squadrons, By Type, Far East Air Forces By Month: Jan through Dec, 1948 8

Table 6 - Tactical Groups and Separate Squadrons, By Type, Pacific Air Command, By Month: Jan through Dec, 1948 9

PART II - AIRCRAFT AND MATERIEL

Introduction 11A

Class Designation of Aircraft 11

Section II - *Procurement*

A. Air Force Aircraft

Table 7 - Airplanes Authorized for USAF Procurement, By Type and Model of Airplane: Fiscal Year 1948 12

Table 8 - Average Unit Cost of USAF Airplanes Authorized for Procurement, By Principal Model: Fiscal Year 1948 13

Table 9 - Factory Acceptances of USAF Cognizance Airplanes, By Type and Model of Airplane: Monthly 1948 14

Table 10 - Airframe Weight of Factory Accepted USAF Cognizance Airplanes, By Type of Airplane: Monthly 1948 15

B. All Military Aircraft (USAF and Navy)

Table 11 - Factory Acceptances of All US Military Airplanes, By Type of Airplane: Monthly 1948 15

Table 12 - Factory Acceptances of All Military Airplanes, By Plant and By Type and Model of Airplane: Monthly 1948 16

Table 13 - Airframe Weight of All Factory Accepted US Military Airplanes, By Type of Airplane: Monthly 1948 18

Table 14 - US Military Airplane Factory Deliveries, By Type of Airplane and By Recipient: Monthly 1948 18

C. Aircraft Engines

Table 15 - Factory Deliveries of All Military Jet-Propelled Aircraft Engines, By Plant, By Model and By Unit Horsepower: 1948 19

Table 16 - Factory Deliveries of All Military Aircraft Engines, By Plant, By Model and By Unit Horsepower: 1948 19

Section III - *On Hand*

Table 17 - Summary of USAF Aircraft On Hand, By Major Air Command - Including Air Force Reserve, Civil Air Patrol and Air National Guard: Monthly 1948 . . . 20

Table 18 - Summary of USAF Aircraft On Hand, for the USAF, The Reserve Forces and Civil Air Patrol, By Command and By Type and Model of Aircraft: End of Each Quarter, 1948 21

Table 19 - Airplanes On Hand in the USAF, By Major Type: Monthly 1948 33

Table 20 - Airplanes On Hand in the USAF, By Type and Principal Model: Monthly 1948 . . . 34

Table 21 - Airplanes On Hand in Continental US, By Type and Principal Model: Monthly 1948 . . . 36

Table 22 - Airplanes On Hand Overseas, By Type and Principal Model: Monthly 1948 38

Table 23 - Airplanes On Hand in the USAF Accountable Inventory, By Type and Principal Model, Showing Gains and Losses: 31 Dec 1947 through 30 June 1948 40

Table 24 - Airplanes On Hand in the USAF Accountable Inventory, By Type and Principal Model, Showing Gains and Losses: 30 Jun 1948 through 31 Dec 1948 42

Table 25 - Cumulative Age Distribution of the USAF Airplane Inventory: As of 30 November 1948 44

Table 26 - Airplanes On Hand in the USAF During 1948: Active and Inactive 45

Table 27 - Value of Aircraft Parts in Inventory and On-Order, By Property Classification and Airplane Manufacturer or Major Component Involved: As of January 1948-January 1949 46

Section IV - *Losses*

Table 28 - Airplane Losses in Continental US and Overseas, By Type of Airplane: Monthly 1948 47

Section V - *Storage*

Table 29 - Aircraft In Storage at Air Materiel Command Installations, in Continental US, By Type of Airplane: Monthly 1948 48

Table 30 - USAF Owned or Leased Bulk Petroleum Storage Capacity, By Area and Product: 3rd and 4th Quarter 1948 49

CONTENTS — Continued

PART III - FLIGHT OPERATIONS
Introduction ... 50A
Section VI - *Flying Time*
- Table 31 - Flying Time of USAF Aircraft, By Command and By Type and Model: 1948 ... 50
- Table 32 - Flying Time of USAF Aircraft During 1948, By Basic Type and Model ... 54
- Table 33 - USAF Flying Time in Continental US, By Type and Model: During 1948 ... 56
- Table 34 - USAF Flying Time Overseas, By Type and Model: During 1948 ... 58
- Table 35 - USAF Flying Time in Air Transport Command (Worldwide), By Type and Model: Jan through Jun 1948 ... 60
- Table 36 - USAF Flying Time in Military Air Transport Service (Worldwide), By Type and Model: Jul through Dec 1948 ... 61

Section VII - *Utilization and Maintenance*
- Table 37 - Utilization and Maintenance of USAF Aircraft, By Command: Monthly 1948 ... 62
- Table 38 - Utilization and Maintenance of USAF Aircraft, By Type and Model and By Type of Flying: During 1948 ... 64

Section VIII - *Aviation Fuel Consumption*
- Table 39 - Aviation Fuel Consumption of USAF Aircraft During 1948, By Command ... 70
- Table 40 - Aviation Fuel Consumption of USAF Aircraft, By Type and Model: During 1948 ... 72

Section IX - *Aircraft Accidents*
- Table 41 - Number and Rate of USAF Aircraft Accidents, By Type and Model of Aircraft: Quarterly 1948 ... 74

PART IV - USAF RESERVE FORCES
Introduction ... 77
Section X - *Air Reserve*
- Table 42 - Airplanes On Hand in the Air Reserve, By Air Force Area and By Type and Model of Airplane: Monthly 1948 ... 78
- Table 43 - Summary of Air Force Reserve Activities - During 1948 ... 80
- Table 44 - Flying Time of Air Force Pilots on Inactive Duty Status - During 1948 ... 80

Section XI - *Air National Guard*
- Table 45 - Airplanes On Hand in Air National Guard, By Air Force Area and State or Territory: Monthly 1948 ... 81
- Table 46 - Airplanes On Hand in Air National Guard, By Type and Model of Airplane: Monthly 1948 ... 84
- Table 47 - Summary of Air National Guard Aircraft Activities - During 1948 ... 86

PART V - MILITARY PERSONNEL
Introduction ... 87
Section XII - *Enlistments*
- Table 48 - Enlistments for USAF By Status as to Prior Service, By Sex, By Month: Jan through Dec, 1948 ... 89
- Table 49 - Enlistments for USAF, By Term of Enlistment, By Sex, By Month: Jan through Dec, 1948 ... 89
- Table 50 - Enlistments for USAF, By Grade, By Race, By Month: Jan through Dec, 1948 ... 90
- Table 51 - WAF Enlistments for USAF, By Status as to Prior Service, and By Term of Enlistment, By Month: Jul through Dec, 1948 ... 91
- Table 52 - WAF Enlistments for the USAF, By Status as to Prior Service, By Grade of Enlistment, By Race, By Month: Jul through Dec, 1948 ... 91
- Table 53 - One Year Enlistments for USAF By Status as to Prior Service, By Race, By Month: Jul through Dec, 1948 ... 92
- Table 54 - Re-enlistments (Other than Negro and Negro) in the Army for ARMAF Duty, By Sex, By Month: Apr through Dec, 1948 ... 92
- Table 55 - Immediate Reenlistments (Other than Negro and Negro) in the Army for ARMAF Duty, By Sex, By Grade, By Month: Jan through Dec, 1948 ... 93

INDEX ... 95-99

FOREWORD

The 1948 edition of the United States Air Force Statistical Digest has been segregated into two separate volumes. Volume I contains statistical data which are classified "Restricted" or are unclassified, whereas Volume II includes information classified as high as "Secret". This publication represents the latter of the two volumes.

The greater portion of the information included in this volume had been classified no higher than "Restricted" in previous editions of the Digest. The change in the classification of this material was made after a security survey, completed during the early part of the year, indicated that the classification of such information should be raised, due to the current relative importance of this type of data to national security.

Another change, made effective with the 1948 edition of the Digest, pertains to the scope of the data included in each of the statistical tables. Although it includes the majority of the tables carried in the 1947 edition, the present issue is unlike that for previous years in that its coverage has been restricted to data for the Calendar Year 1948. In addition, several new tables have been added.

To facilitate the use of this volume, it has been divided into the following parts, each covering a specific phase of USAF activity:

1. Tactical Units
2. Aircraft and Matériel
3. Flight Operations
4. USAF Reserve Forces
5. Military Personnel

The tables in each part are preceded by an introductory statement, giving an indication of the character of the data and new topics introduced.

Sources of the majority of the data are the many published and unpublished records of Statistical Services. The tabulations which were furnished by other offices in Headquarters, USAF or USAF Commands are annotated as to source. Tables containing no source references are those supplied by Statistical Services.

Comments, recommendations and suggestions for future editions of this publication should be addressed to Headquarters, U. S. Air Force, Comptroller, ATTN: Statistical Services, Washington 25, D. C.

GLOSSARY
(Aircraft terminology applicable to statistical data for the calendar year 1948)

ACCEPTANCE, AIRCRAFT
The acceptance of a military type aircraft from production by an authorized representative of the Government. In the case of the USAF, this normally precedes or coincides with delivery. In the case of the Navy, acceptance and delivery are simultaneous.

ACCIDENT, AIRCRAFT
An event, involving one or more military aircraft, that occurs while the aircraft is engaged in any phase of aerial flight including takeoff and landing runs, taxiing, or while the aircraft is on the ground and power plant is in operation (except maintenance operation—servicing, repair, etc.) and which results in death or injury to persons or damage to the aircraft.

ACCIDENT, AIRCRAFT, MAJOR
An accident which results in death or major injury to persons or major damage to the aircraft. Major injury is that which will probably require hospitalization for a period of five or more days or results in unconsciousness, fractures (Except simple finger or toe fractures), lacerations of muscles or which cause hemorrhages, internal lesions and burns involving more than five percent of body surface or involving less than five percent if to the second or third degrees. Major damage includes damage to such parts of the aircraft as landing gear, wings, fuselage, stabilizers and power plant to the extent that the part must undergo major repair or be replaced.

ACCIDENT, AIRCRAFT, MINOR
An accident which results in minor injury to persons or minor damage to the aircraft. Minor injury is less severe than major injury as defined above and requires that military personnel be reported on the daily sick report as sick in quarters or hospital, or in the case of civilian personnel, less of regular working time beyond the work-day on which the accident occurred. Minor damage is such damage as to make the aircraft unsafe for flight but not damage so great as to be classified major damage as defined above.

ACTIVE AIRCRAFT INVENTORY
Includes (1) aircraft being used for defense, tactical, transport and search missions, and for unit or crew training (2) those used for minimum individual training, administrative or staff work and special missions (3) aircraft used for experimental development, and test purposes (except "X" Models) and those being repaired (4) pipeline - such as those undergoing depot maintenance or modifications, or projects excess to command requirements, and grounded awaiting transfer. In addition, active data for January-June 1948 include aircraft on bailment contract, those on loan, "X" prefixed aircraft, and active aircraft in the Air Reserve and CAP.

ADMINISTRATIVE AIRCRAFT
Aircraft being used in AF administrative or staff work.

AIRCRAFT
The term aircraft and all type, model and series designations including prefixes are synonymous with the terminology of heavier-than-air aircraft as used in AF Regulation 65-60, dated 11 June 1948, unless otherwise specifically noted.

AIRCRAFT-CLASS-GIZ
Complete aircraft used for ground instructional purposes.

AIRCRAFT INVENTORY
Includes all heavier-than-air aircraft as defined under "AIRCRAFT" which have been delivered to the USAF, except Class GIZ aircraft.

AIRFRAME
The assembled principal structural components of an aircraft. It includes hull or fuselage, wings, stabilizers, vertical fins, control surfaces, landing gear, nacelles, and (lighter-than-air) envelopes.

AIRFRAME WEIGHT
Empty weight of an airplane less the weight of the following government furnished equipment: engines, propellers, hubs, blades, power control and governors, wheels, brakes, tires and tubes, auxiliary power plant, turbo-superchargers, radio receivers and transmitters, starters, batteries, generators, turrets and power-operated gun mounts.

AIRPLANE
All aircraft except aerial target aircraft and gliders.

AVIATION FUEL CONSUMPTION
The amount of aviation fuel consumed on aircraft flights, including fuel consumed in taxiing, warm-up, etc.

BAILMENT AIRCRAFT
Aircraft assigned to other than a Department of the Air Force activity under bailment contract. Bailment aircraft include the following categories: Bailment for test; for maintenance; for modification and bailment for other purposes. (See table I AFL 150-10).

CLASSIFICATION OF AIRCRAFT
Designation and classification of all aircraft reflected in this publication are in accordance with AF Regulation 65-60. As a general rule, unless otherwise indicated, aircraft data covering the period, Jan-Jun 1948, are classified in accordance with AF regulation 65-60, dated 17 Jun 1947 while data for Jul-Dec 1948 are based upon the revision to this regulation, dated 11 Jun 1948.

BASIC TYPE DESIGNATOR. The type classification is generally based upon the basic type designator or the prefix preceding the basic type designator of each aircraft model. Aircraft are assigned a basic type designator in accordance with the function for which they are basically designed. When a type of aircraft is modified to perform a function other than its basically designed function, the basic type designator is prefixed by the appropriate auxiliary symbol. Aircraft are not redesignated merely on the basis of current usage. The basic type designation consists of one letter, as follows:

A	Amphibious
B*	Bomber
C*	Cargo
F*	Fighter
G*	Glider
H	Rotary Wing (Helicopter)
L*	Liaison
Q*	Target aircraft and Drones
R*	Reconnaissance
S*	Search and Rescue
T*	Trainer
X**	Special Research or Experimental

(* Used as prefix symbol as required)
(** Used as classification symbol as required)

PREFIX SYMBOLS. A prefix symbol is assigned an aircraft model when the aircraft is modified to perform a function (indicated by the prefix) other than its basically designated purpose. As an example of such redesignation, a B-50A aircraft modified as a reconnaissance aircraft is redesignated a RB-50A. An aircraft so redesignated retains this prefix until such time as those features which provided its reconnaissance characteristics are re-

VIII

GLOSSARY

CLASSIFICATION OF AIRCRAFT (Continued)
PREFIX SYMBOLS (Continued)
moved and it is restored to its original basic condition or remodified for an entirely different function.

Prefix "B" is used to designate aircraft modified to function as bomber type aircraft, i.e., the inclusion of a bombardier nose in fighter type aircraft. The addition of external bomb, torpedo or depth-charge carrying devices and dive or skip bombing sighting equipment on any basic type aircraft does not constitute sufficient cause for the redesignation of that aircraft as "B" type.

Prefix "C" is used to designate aircraft specifically modified for cargo use. Basic type aircraft utilized for cargo purposes without modification will not be redesignated with the prefix "C".

Prefix "D" is used to designate those aircraft which are modified to function as director aircraft in conjunction with remotely controlled aircraft or guided missiles (See AFR 58-5).

Prefix "F" is used to designate basic aircraft modified for fighter operations. The addition of rocket launchers on liaison or rotary wing aircraft does not constitute sufficient cause for redesignation as "F" type aircraft.

Prefix "M" is used to designate aircraft modified for use as missiles. (See AFR 58-5).

Prefix "Q" is used to designate basic aircraft modified through the inclusion of special electronic equipment for use as targets or drones.

Prefix "R" is used to designate those basic aircraft which have been so modified as to make them suitable for reconnaissance missions, i.e., weather reconnaissance, photo reconnaissance, etc.

Prefix "S" is used to designate basic aircraft modified through the inclusion of special search electronic equipment, airborne life boats, life rafts, or extensive life saving equipment, etc. This symbol is not used to redesignate those aircraft utilized for air evacuation of litter patients.

Prefix "T" is used to designate those aircraft which have had equipment removed to make them more suitable for training purposes. This symbol also is used to designate those aircraft modified through the inclusion of special training equipment, i.e., navigator trainers, engineer trainers, etc. Aircraft used for training purposes for which authorization to remove equipment has not been granted will not carry the prefix "T". "T" prefixed aircraft is not considered suitable for return to combat status; therefore, the "T" prefix normally will not be authorized to combat potential aircraft.

Prefix "V" is used to designate those aircraft which are modified as staff administrative transports. This includes modified cargo types wherein the modification is not indicated by a series letter. Staff administrative transports include all aircraft with passenger seat, chair, or lounge installations and other accessories other than crew type seats.

CLASSIFICATION SYMBOLS - Aircraft may have any one of the following classification symbols where applicable:

Classification "E" The classification symbol "E" (Exempt) is used to designate those aircraft on special tests or experimental projects by authorized activities and for aircraft on bailment contract work.

Classification "X" The classification "X" symbol is used to designate experimental aircraft and indicates that the item being developed has not progressed to the stage where engineering tests indicate that the item is sufficiently satisfactory to warrant service tests. This classification also is used to designate production aircraft that have been so modified for experi-

CLASSIFICATION OF AIRCRAFT (Continued)
Classification "X" (Continued)
mental or other reasons as to make them permanently unsuitable for an operational or training requirement i.e., the experimental installation of R-4360 engines in B-29 aircraft, the experimental installation of tandem landing gear on B-26 aircraft, etc.

Classification "Y" The classification symbol "Y" is used to designate those aircraft which have the required military characteristics and are of a quantity produced to develop the potentialities of the model. This classification indicates the item has been developed beyond the experimental stage, but is not ready for classification as an adopted item.

Classification "Z" The classification symbol "Z" is used to designate aircraft which are considered by the Chief of Staff, USAF, to be obsolete and for which no further procurement will be made. Obsolete aircraft are those aircraft that are declared unsuitable for their original military purposes or for training purposes.

LINE CLASSIFICATION - The classification of aircraft into first and second line categories is generally determined by the age of the aircraft, purpose for which it was designed and/or modified, and its state of obsolescence indicating no further spare part procurement.

"First-line" Aircraft bearing a basic type designator only are considered as first-line of the type indicated by the basic type designator. Aircraft with a basic type designator preceded by the auxiliary prefix symbols "R" and "S" are considered as first-line of the type indicated by the prefix.

Prefix "T" aircraft procured as trainers are considered as first-line of the trainer type.

Prefix "Y" aircraft being utilized to meet a first-line test requirement (i.e., YF-84, YC-97 and YH-13) are considered as first-line of the type indicated by the basic type designator.

"Second-line" Except for the instances described above, aircraft with a basic type preceded by any other basic type designator authorized to be used as an auxiliary prefix are considered second-line of the type indicated by the prefix. Aircraft with a basic type designator preceded by any other prefix symbol (i.e., "D" and "M"), or classification symbol (i.e., "E", "X", "Y", "Z" and "K") are considered second-line of the type indicated by the basic type designator. Any aircraft bearing the prefix symbol "V" is considered as second-line of the transport type.

COGNIZANCE
Designations used to identify the aircraft of the USAF and the US Navy, respectively.

COMBAT AIRPLANE
Any type of bomber, fighter, reconnaissance or search and rescue airplane.

CONTINENTAL US - or - ZONE OF THE INTERIOR
All operations and items of major USAF commands within the 48 States and the District of Columbia. Normally, data for Military Air Transport Service, Air Force Reserve, Air National Guard and Civil Air Patrol are excluded, unless specifically indicated.

CONVERSIONS AND/OR REDESIGNATIONS
Aircraft converted from one type, model, and series to another, by having changes made (usually structural and mechanical or by installation of additional equipment or different type engines) which result in different characteristics. For example: B-29 to RB-29, etc. Also included are aircraft which are reclassified from first line to second line for non-tactical use.

GLOSSARY

DELIVERY, AIRCRAFT
The final transaction between manufacturer and recipient whereupon the airplane becomes a part of the official inventory.

FATAL AIRCRAFT ACCIDENT
An aircraft accident involving fatal injury to personnel.

FATALITIES (Aircraft accidents)
Fatalities which are the result of an aircraft accident.

FIRST-LINE AIRCRAFT
Aircraft with characteristics and performance which make them suitable to perform the primary missions for which they were produced. It is anticipated that these aircraft normally will not remain in first-line status beyond the period of their first-line life as shown in table IX of AFL 150-10.

FLYABLE INACTIVE AIRCRAFT
Aircraft which are not currently applicable to, required or used for, the accomplishment of any Air Force mission involving flight but which are maintained in readiness for flight in accordance with existing technical orders and which may be flown a maximum of five hours a month.

FLYING ACTIVE AIRCRAFT INVENTORY
Includes only those aircraft which are currently required to fly an appreciable amount. This inventory is the active inventory less those aircraft undergoing depot maintenance or modification, on projects, excess to command requirements, and aircraft grounded awaiting transfer.

FLYING TIME
The aircraft hours flown based on AF Form 1, as reported on AF Form 110A.

GAINS FROM PRODUCTION
Factory deliveries allocated to the United States Air Force during the reporting period.

INACTIVE AIRCRAFT INVENTORY
Includes aircraft which are in storage, excess to USAF requirements, and recommended for reclamation. In addition, inactive data for July-December 1948 include aircraft on bailment contract, and those on loan, "X" prefixed aircraft, and all aircraft in the Air Reserve and CAP.

IN COMMISSION
This means that an aircraft, without additional repair or maintenance, can fly and accomplish the primary mission required by the reporting organization.

MILITARY AIRCRAFT PRODUCTION
All aircraft produced for the USAF, Army, Navy and the National Guard.

MILITARY AIR TRANSPORT SERVICE
As reported herein Military Air Transport Service world-wide operations are for the USAF only and are shown as a separate command where applicable.

MINIMUM INDIVIDUAL TRAINING AIRCRAFT
Aircraft primarily maintained and utilized in minimum individual training (Flying proficiency).

MODIFICATION, AIRCRAFT
Aircraft which are at a depot or with a contractor for the sole purpose of modification. Aircraft

MODIFICATION, AIRCRAFT (Continued)
which are concurrently undergoing normal depot maintenance are not included in this category.

ON HAND
This term denotes inventory on a possession basis

OPERATIONAL AIRCRAFT
Aircraft primarily maintained and utilized for defense, tactical, transport and search missions, and for unit or crew training (including tow target missions and troop carrier unit or crew training).

OVERSEAS
All operations and items of Major USAF Commands outside the Continental US. Normally, data for Military Air Transport Service, Air National Guard and Air Force Reserve are excluded unless specifically indicated.

PIPELINE AIRCRAFT
Includes those aircraft in the following categories: In depot maintenance, in modification, on bailment for modification, on project, excess to command but not yet excess to USAF requirements, those grounded for transfer, those enroute and transient aircraft.

RESERVE FORCES
This term as used herein refers collectively to the Air Force Reserve and the Air National Guard unless otherwise specifically stated.

SECOND-LINE AIRCRAFT
Aircraft whose deficiencies in characteristics, and performance entail a recognized handicap for military use, but which may be used for the purposes for which they were produced, or for other purposes. Normally, these aircraft will have exceeded their first-line life.

SERVICE TEST AND EXPERIMENTAL AIRCRAFT
Includes those aircraft, other than "X" prefixed aircraft, which have been procured or modified for service test purposes ("Y" models) and also those standard production type aircraft which are reported as being used for experimental purposes.

STORAGE AIRCRAFT
Aircraft which are not currently applicable to, required or used for, the accomplishment of any Air Force mission involving flight and which are not maintained in readiness for flight. Includes those aircraft reported in either temporary or cocooned storage.

TACTICAL UNITS
Includes any bomber, fighter, reconnaissance, carrier, rescue, liaison, geodetic control or tow target unit.

TRANSIENT AIRCRAFT
Aircraft undergoing maintenance in a unit of a Major Air Command other than its own.

USAF
This term denotes operations and items of the Regular Air Force Establishment. Normally data for the Air Force Reserve, Air National Guard, Civil Air Patrol, or any other agency associated with the United States Air Force are excluded unless specifically indicated.

PART I
TACTICAL UNITS............................

TACTICAL UNITS

Statistics on the number of tactical groups and separate squadrons presented in the following tables include only those units which were actually activated and/or organized prior to or on the dates shown: i.e., units which had been actually activated and/or organized and for which inactivation or disbandment orders had not been actually accomplished by the dates shown. Activated Units presented in these tables include Record Units.

Record Units presented in the following tables are tactical units as defined above, reporting assigned military strength of approximately one (1) officer and one (1) airmen (and without equipment) whose functions are to maintain records and reports required pending disposition of units, i.e., manning with military personnel when sufficient personnel are available, or to redesignate, reorganize, reassign or inactivate.

Tactical Units are listed by the number of group headquarters and squadrons of Bomber, Fighter, Reconnaissance, and Troop Carrier type and by number of separate squadrons of Photographic Reconnaissance (Special), Liaison, Rescue, Geodetic and Tow Target types. The figures immediately preceding the parentheses indicate the number of group headquarters; figures within the parentheses represent the number of squadrons of the type corresponding to the group; and the figures below the group show the number of separate squadrons.

TABLE 1.-- TACTICAL GROUPS AND SEPARATE SQUADRONS BY TYPE, CONTINENTAL US AND OVERSEAS, BY MONTH: JAN THROUGH DEC, 1948

(Figures are as of the end of the month and include Military Air Transport Service)

	January		February		March		April	
	Activated Units	Record Units	Activated Units	Record Units	Activated Units	Record Units	Activated Units	Record Units
Total US Air Force								
Group - Total a/ b/	70 (210)	15 (41)	70 (210)	15 (41)	70 (210)	15 (41)	70 (210)	15 (41)
Very Heavy Bombardment	21 (63)	8 (24)	21 (63)	8 (24)	21 (63)	8 (24)	21 (63)	8 (24)
Heavy Bombardment	-	-	-	-	-	-	-	-
Medium Bombardment	-	-	-	-	-	-	-	-
Light Bombardment	5 (15)	2 (6)	5 (15)	2 (6)	5 (15)	2 (6)	5 (15)	2 (6)
Fighter	25 (75)	1 (3)	25 (75)	1 (3)	25 (75)	1 (3)	25 (75)	1 (3)
Reconnaissance	9 (27)	2 (4)	9 (27)	2 (4)	9 (27)	2 (4)	9 (27)	2 (4)
Troop Carrier	10 (30)	2 (4)	10 (30)	2 (4)	10 (30)	2 (4)	10 (30)	2 (4)
Separate Squadron - Total a/ b/	18	2	18	2	18	2	18	2
Photo Reconnaissance (Special)	1	-	1	-	1	-	1	-
Liaison	9	2	9	2	9	2	9	2
Rescue	6	-	6	-	6	-	6	-
Geodetic	1	-	1	-	1	-	1	-
Tow Target	1	-	1	-	1	-	1	-
Continental US								
Group - Total a/	43 (115)	12 (32)	43 (116)	12 (32)	44 (120)	12 (32)	43 (116)	12 (32)
Very Heavy Bombardment	15 (45)	5 (15)	15 (45)	5 (15)	16 (48)	5 (15)	16 (48)	5 (15)
Heavy Bombardment	-	-	-	-	-	-	-	-
Medium Bombardment	-	-	-	-	-	-	-	-
Light Bombardment	3 (9)	2 (6)	3 (9)	2 (6)	3 (9)	2 (6)	3 (9)	2 (6)
Fighter	13 (36)	1 (3)	13 (37)	1 (3)	13 (37)	1 (3)	12 (34)	1 (3)
Reconnaissance	7 (13)	2 (4)	7 (13)	2 (4)	7 (13)	2 (4)	7 (13)	2 (4)
Troop Carrier	5 (12)	2 (4)	5 (12)	2 (4)	5 (13)	2 (4)	5 (12)	2 (4)
Separate Squadron - Total a/	9	1	9	1	9	1	9	1
Photo Reconnaissance (Special)	1	-	1	-	1	-	1	-
Liaison	5	1	5	1	5	1	5	1
Rescue	1	-	1	-	1	-	1	-
Geodetic	1	-	1	-	1	-	1	-
Tow Target	1	-	1	-	1	-	1	-
Overseas								
Group - Total b/	27 (95)	3 (9)	27 (94)	3 (9)	26 (90)	3 (9)	27 (94)	3 (9)
Very Heavy Bombardment	6 (18)	3 (9)	6 (18)	3 (9)	5 (15)	3 (9)	5 (15)	3 (9)
Heavy Bombardment	-	-	-	-	-	-	-	-
Medium Bombardment	-	-	-	-	-	-	-	-
Light Bombardment	2 (6)	-	2 (6)	-	2 (6)	-	2 (6)	-
Fighter	12 (39)	-	12 (38)	-	12 (38)	-	13 (41)	-
Reconnaissance	2 (14)	-	2 (14)	-	2 (14)	-	2 (14)	-
Troop Carrier	5 (18)	-	5 (18)	-	5 (17)	-	5 (18)	-
Separate Squadron - Total b/	9	1	9	1	9	1	9	1
Liaison	4	1	4	1	4	1	4	1
Rescue	5	-	5	-	5	-	5	-

a/ Continental US includes units en-route to overseas.

b/ Units en-route to US from overseas are included in the overseas area from which they were en-route.

TABLE I.-- TACTICAL GROUPS AND SEPARATE SQUADRONS BY TYPE, CONTINENTAL US AND OVERSEAS, BY MONTH: JAN THROUGH DEC, 1948, Continued

(Figures are as of the end of the month and include Military Air Transport Service)

Type of Unit	May Activated Units	May Record Units	June Activated Units	June Record Units	July Activated Units	July Record Units	August Activated Units	August Record Units
Total US Air Force								
Group - Total a/ b/	70 (210)	15 (41)	70 (210)	15 (41)	70 (212)	17 (40)	70 (212)	15 (39)
Very Heavy Bombardment	13 (39)	8 (24)	13 (39)	8 (24)	9 (27)	8 (24)	7 (21)	7 (21)
Heavy Bombardment	-	-	-	-	1 (3)	-	1 (3)	-
Medium Bombardment	8 (24)	-	8 (24)	-	11 (35)	-	13 (41)	(2)
Light Bombardment	5 (15)	2 (6)	5 (15)	2 (6)	5 (15)	2 (6)	5 (15)	2 (6)
Fighter	25 (75)	1 (3)	25 (75)	1 (3)	25 (75)	1 (3)	25 (75)	1 (3)
Reconnaissance	9 (27)	2 (4)	9 (27)	2 (4)	9 (27)	3 (3)	9 (27)	2 (3)
Troop Carrier	10 (30)	2 (4)	10 (30)	2 (4)	10 (30)	3 (4)	10 (30)	3 (4)
Separate Squadron - Total a/ b/	18	2	18	2	18	2	17	1
Photo Reconnaissance (Special)	1	-	1	-	1	-	1	-
Liaison	9	2	9	2	9	2	8	1
Rescue	6	-	6	-	6	-	6	-
Geodetic	1	-	1	-	1	-	1	-
Tow Target	1	-	1	-	1	-	1	-
Continental US								
Group - Total a/	44 (119)	12 (32)	43 (117)	12 (32)	41 (111)	13 (31)	41 (111)	11 (30)
Very Heavy Bombardment	9 (27)	5 (15)	9 (27)	5 (15)	5 (15)	5 (15)	4 (12)	4 (12)
Heavy Bombardment	-	-	-	-	1 (3)	-	1 (3)	-
Medium Bombardment	8 (24)	-	7 (21)	-	7 (23)	-	8 (26)	(2)
Light Bombardment	3 (9)	2 (6)	3 (9)	2 (6)	3 (9)	2 (6)	3 (9)	2 (6)
Fighter	12 (34)	1 (3)	12 (34)	1 (3)	13 (37)	1 (3)	13 (37)	1 (3)
Reconnaissance	7 (13)	2 (4)	7 (13)	2 (4)	7 (13)	3 (3)	7 (13)	2 (3)
Troop Carrier	5 (12)	2 (4)	5 (13)	2 (4)	5 (11)	2 (4)	5 (11)	2 (4)
Separate Squadron - Total a/	9	1	9	1	9	1	8	-
Photo Reconnaissance (Special)	1	-	1	-	1	-	1	-
Liaison	5	1	5	1	5	1	4	-
Rescue	1	-	1	-	1	-	1	-
Geodetic	1	-	1	-	1	-	1	-
Tow Target	1	-	1	-	1	-	1	-
Overseas								
Group - Total b/	26 (91)	3 (9)	27 (93)	3 (9)	29 (101)	4 (9)	29 (101)	4 (9)
Very Heavy Bombardment	4 (12)	3 (9)	4 (12)	3 (9)	4 (12)	3 (9)	3 (9)	3 (9)
Heavy Bombardment	-	-	-	-	-	-	-	-
Medium Bombardment	-	-	1 (3)	-	4 (12)	-	5 (15)	-
Light Bombardment	2 (6)	-	2 (6)	-	2 (6)	-	2 (6)	-
Fighter	13 (41)	-	13 (41)	-	12 (38)	-	12 (38)	-
Reconnaissance	2 (14)	-	2 (14)	-	2 (14)	-	2 (14)	-
Troop Carrier	5 (18)	-	5 (17)	-	5 (19)	1 (-)	5 (19)	1 (-)
Separate Squadron - Total b/	9	1	9	1	9	1	9	1
Liaison	4	1	4	1	4	1	4	1
Rescue	5	-	5	-	5	-	5	-

TABLE I.-- TACTICAL GROUPS AND SEPARATE SQUADRONS BY TYPE, CONTINENTAL US AND OVERSEAS, BY MONTH: JAN THROUGH DEC, 1948. Continued

(Figures are as of the end of the month and include Military Air Transport Service)

Type of Unit	September Activated Units	September Record Units	October Activated Units	October Record Units	November Activated Units	November Record Units	December Activated Units	December Record Units
Total US Air Force								
Group - Total a/ b/	61 (188)	5 (15)	58 (180)	-	59 (183)	2 (3)	60 (186)	1
Very Heavy Bombardment	3 (9)	3 (9)	-	-	-	-	-	-
Heavy Bombardment	1 (3)	-	1 (3)	-	1 (3)	-	2 (6)	-
Medium Bombardment	13 (41)	(1)	13 (41)	-	13 (41)	-	13 (41)	-
Light Bombardment	3 (9)	-	3 (9)	-	3 (9)	-	3 (9)	-
Fighter	25 (75)	1 (3)	25 (75)	-	25 (75)	1 (3)	25 (75)	-
Reconnaissance	8 (25)	1 (1)	8 (26)	-	8 (25)	-	8 (25)	-
Troop Carrier	8 (26)	(1)	8 (26)	-	9 (30)	1 (-)	9 (30)	1
Separate Squadron - Total a/ b/	17	1	17	-	17	1	17	1
Photo Reconnaissance (Special)	1	-	1	-	1	-	1	-
Liaison	8	1	8	-	8	1	8	1
Rescue	6	-	6	-	6	-	6	-
Geodetic	1	-	1	-	1	-	1	-
Tow Target	1	-	1	-	1	-	1	-
Continental US								
Group - Total a/	32 (89)	2 (6)	33 (91)	2 (3)	32 (87)	2 (3)	34 (93)	1
Very Heavy Bombardment	-	-	-	-	-	-	-	-
Heavy Bombardment	1 (3)	-	1 (3)	-	1 (3)	-	2 (6)	-
Medium Bombardment	8 (26)	(1)	8 (26)	-	8 (26)	-	9 (29)	-
Light Bombardment	1 (3)	-	1 (3)	-	1 (3)	-	1 (3)	-
Fighter	13 (37)	1 (3)	13 (37)	1 (3)	13 (37)	1 (3)	13 (37)	-
Reconnaissance	6 (11)	1 (1)	6 (12)	1	6 (11)	-	6 (11)	-
Troop Carrier	3 (9)	(1)	4 (10)	1	3 (7)	1 (-)	3 (7)	1
Separate Squadron - Total a/	8	-	8	-	8	-	8	-
Photo Reconnaissance (Special)	1	-	1	-	1	-	1	-
Liaison	4	-	4	-	4	-	4	-
Rescue	1	-	1	-	1	-	1	-
Geodetic	1	-	1	-	1	-	1	-
Tow Target	1	-	1	-	1	-	1	-
Overseas								
Group - Total b/	29 (99)	3 (9)	25 (89)	-	27 (96)	-	26 (93)	-
Very Heavy Bombardment	3 (9)	3 (9)	-	-	-	-	-	-
Heavy Bombardment	-	-	-	-	-	-	-	-
Medium Bombardment	5 (15)	-	5 (15)	-	5 (15)	-	4 (12)	-
Light Bombardment	2 (6)	-	2 (6)	-	2 (6)	-	2 (6)	-
Fighter	12 (38)	-	12 (38)	-	12 (38)	-	12 (38)	-
Reconnaissance	2 (14)	-	2 (14)	-	2 (14)	-	2 (14)	-
Troop Carrier	5 (17)	-	4 (16)	-	6 (23)	-	6 (23)	-
Separate Squadron - Total b/	9	1	9	1	9	1	9	1
Liaison	4	1	4	1	4	1	4	1
Rescue	5	-	5	-	5	-	5	-

TABLE 2. -- TACTICAL GROUPS AND SEPARATE SQUADRONS, BY TYPE, US AIR FORCES IN EUROPE, BY MONTH: JAN THROUGH DEC, 1948

(Figures are as of the end of the month)

Type of Unit	January Activated Units	January Record Units	February Activated Units	February Record Units	March Activated Units	March Record Units
Group - Total	3 (10)	-	3 (10)	-	3 (10)	-
Medium Bombardment	-	-	-	-	-	-
Fighter	1 (3)	-	1 (3)	-	1 (3)	-
Reconnaissance	(1)	-	(1)	-	(1)	-
Troop Carrier	2 (6)	-	2 (6)	-	2 (6)	-
Separate Squadron - Total	1	1	1	1	1	1
Liaison	1	1	1	1	1	1

Type of Unit	April Activated Units	April Record Units	May Activated Units	May Record Units	June Activated Units	June Record Units
Group - Total	3 (10)	-	3 (10)	-	3 (10)	-
Medium Bombardment	-	-	-	-	-	-
Fighter	1 (3)	-	1 (3)	-	1 (3)	-
Reconnaissance	(1)	-	(1)	-	(1)	-
Troop Carrier	2 (6)	-	2 (6)	-	2 (6)	-
Separate Squadron - Total	1	1	1	1	1	1
Liaison	1	1	1	1	1	1

Type of Unit	July Activated Units	July Record Units	August Activated Units	August Record Units	September Activated Units	September Record Units
Group - Total	6 (23)	-	7 (25)	-	7 (23)	-
Medium Bombardment	3 (9)	-	3 (9)	-	3 (9)	-
Fighter	1 (3)	-	2 (6)	-	2 (6)	-
Reconnaissance	(1)	-	(1)	-	(1)	-
Troop Carrier	2 (10)	-	2 (9)	-	2 (7)	-
Separate Squadron - Total	1	1	1	1	1	1
Liaison	1	1	1	1	1	1

Type of Unit	October Activated Units	October Record Units	November Activated Units	November Record Units	December Activated Units	December Record Units
Group - Total	8 (26)	-	10 (33)	-	10 (33)	-
Medium Bombardment	3 (9)	-	3 (9)	-	3 (9)	-
Fighter	2 (6)	-	2 (6)	-	2 (6)	-
Reconnaissance	(1)	-	(1)	-	(1)	-
Troop Carrier	3 (10)	-	5 (17)	-	5 (17)	-
Separate Squadron - Total	1	1	1	1	1	1
Liaison	1	1	1	1	1	1

TABLE 3. -- TACTICAL GROUPS AND SEPARATE SQUADRONS, BY TYPE, CARIBBEAN AIR COMMAND, BY MONTH: JAN THROUGH DEC, 1948

(Figures are as of the end of the month and include Military Air Transport Service)

Type of Unit	January Activated Units	January Record Units	February Activated Units	February Record Units	March Activated Units	March Record Units
Group - Total	2 (9)	-	2 (9)	-	2 (9)	-
Fighter	1 (4)	-	1 (4)	-	1 (4)	-
Reconnaissance	(3)	-	(3)	-	(3)	-
Troop Carrier	1 (2)	-	1 (2)	-	1 (2)	-
Separate Squadron - Total	2	-	2	-	2	-
Liaison	1	-	1	-	1	-
Rescue	1	-	1	-	1	-

Type of Unit	April Activated Units	April Record Units	May Activated Units	May Record Units	June Activated Units	June Record Units
Group - Total	2 (9)	-	2 (9)	-	2 (9)	-
Fighter	1 (4)	-	1 (4)	-	1 (4)	-
Reconnaissance	(3)	-	(3)	-	(3)	-
Troop Carrier	1 (2)	-	1 (2)	-	1 (2)	-
Separate Squadron - Total	2	-	2	-	2	-
Liaison	1	-	1	-	1	-
Rescue	1	-	1	-	1	-

Type of Unit	July Activated Units	July Record Units	August Activated Units	August Record Units	September Activated Units	September Record Units
Group - Total	2 (8)	1	1 (6)	1	1 (6)	-
Fighter	1 (4)	-	(1)	-	(1)	-
Reconnaissance	(3)	-	(3)	-	(3)	-
Troop Carrier	1 (1)	1	1 (2)	1	1 (2)	-
Separate Squadron - Total	2	-	2	-	2	-
Liaison	1	-	1	-	1	-
Rescue	1	-	1	-	1	-

Type of Unit	October Activated Units	October Record Units	November Activated Units	November Record Units	December Activated Units	December Record Units
Group - Total	(5)	-	(5)	-	(5)	-
Fighter	(1)	-	(1)	-	(1)	-
Reconnaissance	(3)	-	(3)	-	(3)	-
Troop Carrier	(1)	-	(1)	-	(1)	-
Separate Squadron - Total	2	-	2	-	2	-
Liaison	1	-	1	-	1	-
Rescue	1	-	1	-	1	-

TABLE 4.—TACTICAL GROUPS AND SEPARATE SQUADRONS, BY TYPE, ALASKAN AIR COMMAND, BY MONTH JAN THROUGH DEC, 1948

(Figures are as of the end of the month and include Military Air Transport Service)

Type of Units	January Activated Units	January Record Units	February Activated Units	February Record Units	March Activated Units	March Record Units	April Activated Units	April Record Units	May Activated Units	May Record Units	June Activated Units	June Record Units
Group - Total	2 (13)	-	2 (11)	-	1 (7)	-	2 (11)	-	2 (11)	-	2 (10)	-
Very Heavy Bombardment	1 (3)	-	1 (3)	-	-	-	-	-	-	-	-	-
Fighter	1 (5)	-	1 (4)	-	1 (4)	-	2 (7)	-	2 (7)	-	2 (7)	-
Reconnaissance	(2)	-	(2)	-	(2)	-	(2)	-	(2)	-	(2)	-
Troop Carrier	(2)	-	(2)	-	(1)	-	(2)	-	(2)	-	(1)	-
Separate Squadron - Total	1	-	1	-	1	-	1	-	1	-	1	-
Rescue	1	-	1	-	1	-	1	-	1	-	1	-

Type of Units	July Activated Units	July Record Units	August Activated Units	August Record Units	September Activated Units	September Record Units	October Activated Units	October Record Units	November Activated Units	November Record Units	December Activated Units	December Record Units
Group - Total	1 (7)	-	1 (7)	-	1 (7)	-	1 (7)	-	1 (7)	-	1 (7)	-
Fighter	1 (4)	-	1 (4)	-	1 (4)	-	1 (4)	-	1 (4)	-	1 (4)	-
Reconnaissance	(2)	-	(2)	-	(2)	-	(2)	-	(2)	-	(2)	-
Troop Carrier	(1)	-	(1)	-	(1)	-	(1)	-	(1)	-	(1)	-
Separate Squadron - Total	1	-	1	-	1	-	1	-	1	-	1	-
Rescue	1	-	1	-	1	-	1	-	1	-	1	-

847201 O - 49 - 2

TABLE 5. -- TACTICAL GROUPS AND SEPARATE SQUADRONS, BY TYPE, FAR EAST AIR FORCES, BY MONTH, JAN THROUGH DEC, 1948

(Figures are as of the end of the month and include Military Air Transport Service)

Type of Unit	January Activated Units	January Record Units	February Activated Units	February Record Units	March Activated Units	March Record Units
Group - Total	19 (60)	3 (9)	19 (60)	3 (9)	19 (60)	3 (9)
Very Heavy Bombardment	5 (15)	3 (9)	5 (15)	3 (9)	5 (15)	3 (9)
Medium Bombardment	-	-	-	-	-	-
Light Bombardment	2 (6)	-	2 (6)	-	2 (6)	-
Fighter	8 (24)	-	8 (24)	-	8 (24)	-
Reconnaissance	2 (8)	-	2 (8)	-	2 (8)	-
Troop Carrier	2 (7)	-	2 (7)	-	2 (7)	-
Separate Squadron - Total	5	-	5	-	5	-
Liaison	2	-	2	-	2	-
Rescue	3	-	3	-	3	-

Type of Unit	April Activated Units	April Record Units	May Activated Units	May Record Units	June Activated Units	June Record Units
Group - Total	19 (60)	3 (9)	18 (57)	3 (9)	19 (60)	3 (9)
Very Heavy Bombardment	5 (15)	3 (9)	4 (12)	3 (9)	4 (12)	3 (9)
Medium Bombardment	-	-	-	-	1 (3)	-
Light Bombardment	2 (6)	-	2 (6)	-	2 (6)	-
Fighter	8 (24)	-	8 (24)	-	8 (24)	-
Reconnaissance	2 (8)	-	2 (8)	-	2 (8)	-
Troop Carrier	2 (7)	-	2 (7)	-	2 (7)	-
Separate Squadron - Total	5	-	5	-	5	-
Liaison	2	-	2	-	2	-
Rescue	3	-	3	-	3	-

Type of Unit	July Activated Units	July Record Units	August Activated Units	August Record Units	September Activated Units	September Record Units
Group - Total	19 (60)	3 (9)	19 (60)	3 (9)	19 (60)	3 (9)
Very Heavy Bombardment	4 (12)	3 (9)	3 (9)	3 (9)	3 (9)	3 (9)
Medium Bombardment	1 (3)	-	2 (6)	-	2 (6)	-
Light Bombardment	2 (6)	-	2 (6)	-	2 (6)	-
Fighter	8 (24)	-	8 (24)	-	8 (24)	-
Reconnaissance	2 (8)	-	2 (8)	-	2 (8)	-
Troop Carrier	2 (7)	-	2 (7)	-	2 (7)	-
Separate Squadron - Total	5	-	5	-	5	-
Liaison	2	-	2	-	2	-
Rescue	3	-	3	-	3	-

Type of Unit	October Activated Units	October Record Units	November Activated Units	November Record Units	December Activated Units	December Record Units
Group - Total	15 (48)	-	15 (48)	-	14 (45)	-
Very Heavy Bombardment	-	-	-	-	-	-
Medium Bombardment	2 (6)	-	2 (6)	-	1 (3)	-
Light Bombardment	2 (6)	-	2 (6)	-	2 (6)	-
Fighter	8 (24)	-	8 (24)	-	8 (24)	-
Reconnaissance	2 (8)	-	2 (8)	-	2 (8)	-
Troop Carrier	1 (4)	-	1 (4)	-	1 (4)	-
Separate Squadron - Total	5	-	5	-	5	-
Liaison	2	-	2	-	2	-
Rescue	3	-	3	-	3	-

TABLE 6. -- TACTICAL GROUPS AND SEPARATE SQUADRONS, BY TYPE, PACIFIC AIR COMMAND, BY MONTH: JAN THROUGH DEC, 1948

(Figures are as of the end of the month and include Military Air Transport Service)

Type of Unit	January		February		March		April		May		June	
	Activated Units	Record Units	Activated Units	Record Units	Activated Units	Record Units	Activated Units	Record Units	Activated Units	Record Units	Activated Units	Record Units
Group - Total	1 (4)	-	1 (4)	-	1 (4)	-	1 (4)	-	1 (4)	-	1 (4)	-
Fighter	1 (3)	-	1 (3)	-	1 (3)	-	1 (3)	-	1 (3)	-	1 (3)	-
Troop Carrier	(1)	-	(1)	-	(1)	-	(1)	-	(1)	-	(1)	-

	July		August		September		October		November		December	
	Activated Units	Record Units	Activated Units	Record Units	Activated Units	Record Units	Activated Units	Record Units	Activated Units	Record Units	Activated Units	Record Units
Group - Total	1 (3)	-	1 (3)	-	1 (3)	-	1 (3)	-	1 (3)	-	1 (3)	-
Fighter	1 (3)	-	1 (3)	-	1 (3)	-	1 (3)	-	1 (3)	1	1 (3)	-

PART II
AIRCRAFT AND MATERIEL............

AIRCRAFT AND MATERIEL

The tables included in this section provide summary data covering the procurement, production, inventory, status, deployment, and disposition of USAF aircraft, and similar information on other major items of materiel in the USAF. Unlike other issues, the tables presented herein are limited to data covering the Calender Year 1948.

As a result of a major revision of Air Force Regulation 65-60; subject "Modification, Classification, Designation and Redesignation of Heavier-than-air Aircraft", published 11 June 1948, a major change was made in the type, model, series designation of all USAF aircraft. The more important provisions of the revised directive are summarized in the Glossary (Pages VIII and IX). For reporting and accounting purposes, the required changeover to the new type, model, series designations was made effective 1 July 1948. This change in the classification and designation of USAF aircraft has affected a majority of the tables included in this section. In order to reflect the basic information under the classification system in existence during each half of the year and at the same time enable the computation of desired summary totals, aircraft data reflected herein for the year 1948 have been segregated and presented in two separate tabulations, each covering a one-half year period. Data for the period, January-June, are shown in one tabulation under the old type, model, series designations, while those covering the period, July-December, are reflected in a separate tabulation under the new designations. This has been done in all cases where the required designation change has affected the information presented in the tables.

Another major change affecting tables included in this section pertains to the classification of aircraft into "Active" and "Inactive" categories for aircraft inventory accounting purposes. A change was effected in these classification concepts on 1 July 1948 in conjunction with the issuance of an executive order limiting the size of the USAF "Active" Aircraft Inventory. This involved the elimination from the USAF "Active" concept of Reserve Forces and Civilian Air Patrol aircraft, aircraft reported on loan and on bailment contract, and all "X" prefixed aircraft. These categories were added to storage aircraft, those excess to USAF requirements, and aircraft recommended for reclamation to comprise the new "inactive" inventory concept. In all tables affected thereby, this changeover is reflected in the manner and as of the time it occurred. The pertinent data have been annotated accordingly.

Those tables presenting a Command breakdown have been revised to reflect the major reorganizations which took effect during the year, such as the consolidation of the Air Defense and Tactical Air Commands into the Continental Air Command, the creation of the Military Air Transport Service (MATS), etc.

Due to the emphasis placed upon "Operation Vittles" during 1948, information pertaining to this activity has been segregated and presented separately, wherever possible.

In order to reflect aircraft inventory for overseas commands in the same manner as that for the Continental U. S., the separate inventory tables for overseas major commands have been consolidated into one table.

Among the new tables included in this section are:

    Summary of Aircraft on Hand, By Major Air Command-Including Air Force Reserve, Civil Air Patrol and Air National Guard: Monthly 1948

    Summary of USAF Aircraft on Hand-Including Air Force Reserve and Civil Air Patrol, By Command and By Type and Model of Aircraft: Quarterly 1948

    Cumulative Age Distribution of the USAF Airplane Inventory: As of 30 November 1948

    Value of Aircraft Parts in Inventory and On-Order, By Property Classification and Airplane Manufacturer or Major Component Involved: As of Jan 1949

    USAF Owned or Leased Bulk Petroleum Storage Capacity, By Area and Product: 3RD and 4TH Quarter, 1948

TABLE 7.-- AIRPLANES AUTHORIZED FOR USAF PROCUREMENT, BY TYPE AND MODEL OF AIRPLANE: FISCAL YEAR 1948

(Includes experimental airplanes.)

Type and Model	1948
Total	965
Medium Bomber	
B-50D	82
Light Bomber	
B-45C	43
Fighter - Total	344
P-84D	154
P-86A	188
P-86C a/	2
Cargo - Total	120
C-97A	27
C-121A	9
VC-121B	1
C-124A	1
C-82A	20
C-119B	36
XC-120	1
YC-125A	13
YC-125B	10
YC-122	2
Trainer	
TF-80C	28
Liaison - Total	224
L-16B b/	100
L-17B b/	124
Rotary Wing - Total	104
R-5G	39
R-13B b/	65
Search and Rescue	
SA-16A	20

a/ P-86C changed to F-93A, 1 July 1948.
b/ Procured for Army Field Forces.

Source: Cost Control and Analysis Office, Comptroller's Department, Hq. Air Materiel Command.

TABLE 8. -- AVERAGE UNIT COST OF USAF AIRPLANES AUTHORIZED FOR PROCUREMENT, BY PRINCIPAL MODEL-FISCAL YEAR 1948

Note:—Average cost per airplane is the weighted average on all programs approved during a designated fiscal year and represents the estimated cost of a complete airplane ready for flyaway, including factory installed ordnance and radio equipment. Costs exclude equipment installed at modification centers and airplane spare parts. Unit costs reflect renegotiation of contracts only to the extent of reductions in contract prices for future deliveries but do not reflect reductions in price effected by cash refunds.

Type and Model	Number of Aircraft	Unit Cost
Medium Bomber		
B-50	82	$1,228,469
Light Bomber		
B-45C	43	1,296,245
Fighter		
F-48D	174	153,144
P-86A	168	257,801
P-86C	2	a/
Cargo		
C-97A	27	1,145,258
C-121A	9	1,152,330
VC-121B	1	1,152,330
C-124	1	2,813,867
C-82A	20	287,525
C-119B	36	736,533
XC-120	1	3,929,615
YC-125A	13	299,628
YC-125B	10	306,418
YC-122	2	a/
Trainer		
TF-80C	28	197,971
Liaison		
L-16B	100	2,193
L-17B	124	10,000
Rotary Wing		
R-5G	39	87,315
R-13B	65	27,044
Search and Rescue		
SA-16A	20	612,488

a/ Not Available.

Source: Cost Control and Analysis Office, Comptroller's Department, Hq. Air Materiel Command.

TABLE 9 .-- FACTORY ACCEPTANCES OF USAF COGNIZANCE AIRPLANES, BY TYPE AND MODEL OF AIRPLANE: MONTHLY, 1948

(Includes experimental airplanes.)

Type and Model	1948 Total	Jan	Feb	Mar	Apr	May	Jun	Jul	Aug	Sep	Oct	Nov	Dec
Total	1,425	70	91	162	76	60	143	101	145	163	108	121	185
Bomber - Total	142	7	8	-	2	6	16	14	15	20	7	19	27
B-35	2	-	-	-	-	-	-	-	-	1	-	-	1
B-36	39	-	-	-	-	1	6	5	4	5	-	6	12
B-43	1	-	-	-	1	-	-	-	-	-	-	-	-
B-45	23	-	-	-	1	-	3	3	4	7	1	1	3
B-47	1	-	-	-	-	-	-	-	-	-	-	-	1
B-48	2	-	-	-	-	-	1	-	-	-	-	2	-
B-49	1	-	-	-	-	-	1	-	-	-	-	-	-
B-50	73	7	8	-	1	5	6	6	7	7	6	10	10
Fighter - Total	869	36	61	36	40	43	117	75	111	122	80	74	74
F-56	1	-	-	-	-	1	-	-	-	-	-	-	-
F-80	257	21	8	1	4	6	28	21	66	38	20	21	23
F-82	230	2	3	-	5	17	46	22	18	51	29	29	8
F-84	363	13	50	35	30	17	43	30	25	30	30	24	36
F-86	17	-	-	-	1	2	-	2	2	3	1	-	6
F-87	1	-	-	-	-	-	-	-	-	-	-	-	1
Reconnaissance - Total	3	-	-	1	-	-	-	1	-	-	-	1	-
R-11	1	-	-	1	-	-	-	-	-	-	-	-	-
R-12	2	-	-	-	-	-	-	1	-	-	-	1	-
Special Research - Total	2	-	-	-	2	-	-	-	-	-	-	-	-
X-1	2	-	-	-	2	-	-	-	-	-	-	-	-
Transport - Total	61	6	7	8	7	8	6	6	6	2	-	1	4
C-82	51	6	6	6	7	7	5	6	6	2	-	-	-
C-97	4	-	1	2	-	-	-	-	-	-	-	-	1
C-112	1	-	-	-	-	-	1	-	-	-	-	-	-
C-119	1	-	-	-	-	1	-	-	-	-	-	-	-
C-121	4	-	-	-	-	-	-	-	-	-	-	1	3
Trainer - Total	20	-	-	-	-	-	-	-	-	3	3	4	5	5
TF-80	20	-	-	-	-	-	-	-	-	3	3	4	5	5
Communications - Total	328	21	15	117	24	2	4	5	10	16	17	21	75
H-5	30	-	-	4	3	3	2	3	3	3	3	3	3
H-10	1	-	-	-	-	-	1	-	-	-	-	-	-
H-12	2	-	-	-	-	-	1	1	-	-	-	-	-
H-13	59	-	-	-	-	-	-	1	7	13	14	11	13
L-13	67	20	15	19	13	-	-	-	-	-	-	-	-
L-15	3	-	-	-	2	-	-	-	-	-	-	-	1
L-16	101	1	-	94	6	-	-	-	-	-	-	-	-
L-17	65	-	-	-	-	-	-	-	-	-	-	7	58

TABLE 10.-- AIRFRAME WEIGHT OF FACTORY ACCEPTED USAF COGNIZANCE AIRPLANES, BY TYPE AIRPLANE: MONTHLY, 1948

(Includes experimental airplanes. In thousands of pounds.)

Month	Total 1948	Heavy Bomber	Medium Bomber	Light Bomber	Fighter	Reconnaissance	Transport	Trainer	Communications	Special Research
Total	16,854.2	3,600.6	4,018.1	713.2	6,321.7	127.0	1,567.1	116.0	381.9	8.6
Jan	711.7	-	352.1	-	207.1	-	126.0	-	26.5	-
Feb	981.9	-	402.4	-	385.3	-	174.7	-	19.5	-
Mar	562.0	-	-	-	225.5	27.4	223.4	-	85.7	-
Apr	566.7	-	50.3	46.6	269.8	-	159.8	-	31.6	8.6
May	872.2	91.6	251.5	-	333.9	-	186.5	-	8.7	-
Jun	2,061.8	543.6	363.5	90.9	900.7	-	148.7	-	14.4	-
Jul	1,604.5	458.0	301.8	90.9	552.4	49.8	139.2	-	12.4	-
Aug	1,761.1	366.4	352.1	121.6	747.7	-	139.2	17.7	16.4	-
Sep	2,135.2	458.0	406.6	212.5	971.0	-	46.4	17.7	23.0	-
Oct	1,002.0	-	301.8	30.7	621.8	-	-	23.6	24.1	-
Nov	1,920.1	561.0	598.6	30.0	580.8	49.8	42.5	28.5	28.9	-
Dec	2,675.0	1,122.0	637.4	90.0	525.7	-	180.7	28.5	90.7	-

TABLE 11.-- FACTORY ACCEPTANCES OF ALL US MILITARY AIRPLANES BY TYPE OF AIRPLANE: MONTHLY 1948

(Includes experimental airplanes.)

Month	Total 1948	Heavy Bomber	Medium Bomber	Light Bomber	Fighter	Reconnaissance	Transport	Trainer	Communications	Special Research
Total	2,533	39	79	442	1,488	12	61	23	387	2
Jan	142	-	7	28	70	-	6	1	30	-
Feb	156	-	8	15	105	-	7	-	21	-
Mar	277	-	-	12	134	2	8	-	121	-
Apr	167	-	1	24	100	6	7	1	26	2
May	141	1	5	29	92	-	8	1	5	-
Jun	229	6	7	36	166	-	6	-	8	-
Jul	201	5	6	43	132	1	6	-	8	-
Aug	269	4	7	59	175	2	6	3	13	-
Sep	277	5	8	65	175	-	2	3	19	-
Oct	204	-	6	48	124	-	-	4	22	-
Nov	215	6	12	50	111	1	1	5	29	-
Dec	255	12	12	33	104	-	4	5	85	-

TABLE 12.-- FACTORY ACCEPTANCES OF ALL MILITARY AIRPLANES, BY PLANT AND BY TYPE AND MODEL OF AIRPLANE: MONTHLY 1948

Note:--Includes experimental airplanes. USAF Cognizance production is shown by model; Navy Cognizance by type.

Plant, Type and Model	Total 1948	Jan	Feb	Mar	Apr	May	Jun	Jul	Aug	Sep	Oct	Nov	Dec
Total	2,533	142	156	277	167	141	229	201	269	277	204	215	255
Aeronca: Middletown, Ohio													
USAF - L-16	101	1	-	94	6	-	-	-	-	-	-	-	-
Bell: Buffalo, N.Y.													
USAF - X-1	2	-	-	-	2	-	-	-	-	-	-	-	-
H-12	2	-	-	-	-	-	1	1	-	-	-	-	-
H-13	59	-	-	-	-	-	-	1	7	13	14	11	13
Navy - Communication	12	4	4	3	1	-	-	-	-	-	-	-	-
Boeing: Seattle, Wash.													
USAF - B-47	1	-	-	-	-	-	-	-	-	-	-	-	1
B-50	73	7	8	-	1	5	6	6	7	7	6	10	10
C-97	4	-	1	2	-	-	-	-	-	-	-	-	1
Boeing: Wichita, Kansas													
USAF - L-15	3	-	-	-	2	-	-	-	-	-	-	-	1
Chance Vought: Stratford, Conn.													
Navy - Fighter	256	15	25	41	29	21	22	22	22	22	22	12	3
Consol-Vultee: Ft. Worth, Texas													
USAF - B-36	39	-	-	-	-	1	6	5	4	5	-	6	12
Consol-Vultee: San Diego, Calif.													
USAF - L-13	67	20	15	19	13	-	-	-	-	-	-	-	-
Curtiss-Wright: Columbus, Ohio													
USAF - F-87	1	-	-	-	-	-	-	-	-	-	-	-	1
Navy - Reconnaissance	1	-	-	1	-	-	-	-	-	-	-	-	-
Douglas: El Segundo, Calif.													
Navy - Light Bomber	230	6	-	-	9	19	14	24	40	40	30	34	14
Fighter	1	-	-	1	-	-	-	-	-	-	-	-	-
Douglas: Santa Monica, Calif.													
USAF - B-43	1	-	-	-	1	-	-	-	-	-	-	-	-
C-112	1	-	-	-	-	-	1	-	-	-	-	-	-
EDO: College Point, N.Y.													
Navy - Reconnaissance	8	-	-	-	6	-	-	-	2	-	-	-	-
Trainer	2	1	-	-	-	1	-	-	-	-	-	-	-
Fairchild: Hagerstown, Md.													
USAF - C-82	51	6	6	6	7	7	5	6	6	2	-	-	-
C-119	1	-	-	-	-	1	-	-	-	-	-	-	-
Navy - Trainer	1	-	-	-	1	-	-	-	-	-	-	-	-
Hughes: Culver City, Calif.													
USAF - R-11	1	-	-	1	-	-	-	-	-	-	-	-	-
Grumman: Bethpage, N.Y.													
Navy - Fighter	307	11	2	43	25	24	27	35	41	31	22	23	23
Kellett: Phila., Pa.													
USAF - H-10	1	-	-	-	-	-	1	-	-	-	-	-	-
Lockheed: Burbank, Calif.													
USAF - F-80	257	21	8	1	4	6	28	21	66	38	20	21	23
TF-80	20	-	-	-	-	-	-	-	3	3	4	5	5
C-121	4	-	-	-	-	-	-	-	-	-	-	1	3
Navy - Patrol Bomber	74	7	6	6	7	3	8	7	6	7	5	6	6

TABLE 12.-- FACTORY ACCEPTANCES OF ALL MILITARY AIRPLANES, BY PLANT AND BY TYPE AND MODEL OF AIRPLANE: MONTHLY 1948--Continued

Plant, Type and Model	Total 1948	Jan	Feb	Mar	Apr	May	Jun	Jul	Aug	Sep	Oct	Nov	Dec
Martin: Baltimore, Md													
USAF - B-48	2	-	-	-	-	-	-	-	-	-	-	2	-
Navy - Patrol Bomber	30	-	-	-	1	2	7	3	4	3	3	3	4
Light Bomber	84	15	9	6	5	5	4	6	5	8	9	6	6
McDonnell: St. Louis, Missouri													
Navy - Fighter	33	3	7	8	4	4	-	-	1	-	-	2	4
North American: Englewood, Calif													
USAF - F-82	230	2	3	-	5	17	46	22	18	51	29	29	8
F-86	17	-	-	-	1	2	-	2	2	3	1	-	6
Navy - Fighter	22	5	10	5	2	-	-	-	-	-	-	-	-
North American: Long Beach, Calif													
USAF - B-45	23	-	-	-	1	-	3	3	4	7	1	1	3
Northrop: Hawthorne, Calif													
USAF - B-35	2	-	-	-	-	-	-	-	-	1	-	-	1
B-49	1	-	-	-	-	-	1	-	-	-	-	-	-
F-56	1	-	-	-	-	1	-	-	-	-	-	-	-
Piasecki: Morton, Pa													
Navy - Communication	15	1	-	-	-	-	2	-	-	-	2	4	6
Republic: Farmingdale, N Y													
USAF - F-84	363	13	50	35	30	17	43	30	25	30	30	24	36
R-12	2	-	-	-	-	-	-	1	-	-	-	1	-
Ryan: San Diego, Calif													
USAF - L-17	65	-	-	-	-	-	-	-	-	-	-	7	58
Sikorsky: Bridgeport, Conn													
USAF - H-5	30	-	-	4	3	3	2	3	3	3	3	3	3
Navy - Communication	32	4	2	1	1	2	2	3	3	3	3	4	4

TABLE 13 .-- AIRFRAME WEIGHT OF ALL FACTORY ACCEPTED US MILITARY AIRPLANES, BY TYPE OF AIRPLANE: MONTHLY, 1948

(Includes experimental airplanes. In thousands of pounds)

Month	Total 1948	Heavy Bomber	Medium Bomber	Light Bomber	Fighter	Reconnaissance	Transport	Trainer	Communications	Special Research
Total ..	25,123.6	3,600.6	4,050.3	5,604.4	9,475.3	150.7	1,567.1	123.0	543.6	8.6
Jan ..	1,253.6	-	352.1	340.3	386.4	-	126.0	2.5	46.3	-
Feb ..	1,464.8	-	402.4	222.0	636.2	-	174.7	-	29.5	-
Mar ..	1,267.7	-	-	193.7	727.3	31.2	223.4	-	92.1	-
Apr ..	1,195.3	-	50.3	343.5	580.7	14.7	159.8	2.0	35.7	8.6
May ..	1,425.6	91.6	251.5	298.8	580.3	-	186.5	2.5	14.4	-
Jun ..	2,837.0	543.6	395.7	576.1	1,146.8	-	148.7	-	26.1	-
Jul ..	2,357.3	458.0	301.8	553.6	833.9	49.8	139.2	-	21.0	-
Aug ..	2,660.1	366.4	352.1	693.6	1,060.9	5.2	139.2	17.7	25.0	-
Sep ..	3,002.6	458.0	406.6	806.8	1,235.5	-	46.4	17.7	31.6	-
Oct ..	1,738.0	-	301.8	523.5	848.6	-	-	23.6	40.5	-
Nov ..	2,652.4	561.0	598.6	548.8	767.3	49.8	42.5	28.5	55.9	-
Dec ..	3,269.2	1,122.0	637.4	503.7	671.4	-	180.7	28.5	125.5	-

TABLE 14 .-- US MILITARY AIRPLANE FACTORY DELIVERIES, BY TYPE OF AIRPLANE AND BY RECIPIENT: MONTHLY, 1948

Note:--Includes experimental airplanes. Subsequent reallocations are not reflected.

Type of Airplane and Recipient	Total	Jan	Feb	Mar	Apr	May	Jun	Jul	Aug	Sep	Oct	Nov	Dec
Total	2,437	153	153	256	158	127	187	228	230	287	230	201	227
USAF	1,010	79	88	57	51	41	96	112	95	128	93	72	98
US Navy.	1,158	72	65	115	91	81	86	108	124	144	106	96	70
Air National Guard	89	-	-	-	-	5	5	7	10	2	17	20	23
Army Field Forces.	177	-	-	84	16	-	-	1	1	13	14	13	35
National Guard Ground.	3	2	-	-	-	-	-	-	-	-	-	-	1
Heavy Bomber - Total	39	-	-	-	-	-	4	7	4	5	1	4	14
USAF	39	-	-	-	-	-	4	7	4	5	1	4	14
Medium Bomber - Total.	77	3	6	6	1	4	5	7	6	10	5	11	13
USAF	76	3	6	6	1	4	4	7	6	10	5	11	13
US Navy.	1	-	-	-	-	-	1	-	-	-	-	-	-
Light Bomber - Total	441	28	15	12	24	29	34	43	59	64	50	49	34
USAF	24	-	-	-	2	-	2	3	4	6	3	-	4
US Navy.	417	28	15	12	22	29	32	40	55	58	47	49	30
Fighter - Total	1,471	83	110	137	97	77	129	149	149	182	143	107	108
USAF	713	49	66	39	37	23	75	77	75	97	72	48	55
US Navy.	669	34	44	98	60	49	49	65	64	83	54	39	30
Air National Guard	89	-	-	-	-	5	5	7	10	2	17	20	23
Reconnaissance - Total	12	-	-	1	7	-	-	1	2	-	-	1	-
USAF	3	-	-	1	1	-	-	1	-	-	-	1	-
US Navy.	9	-	-	-	6	-	-	-	2	-	-	-	-
Transport - Total.	63	6	6	6	7	6	7	10	5	5	2	1	2
USAF	63	6	6	6	7	6	7	10	5	5	2	1	2
Trainer - Total.	23	1	-	-	1	1	-	-	-	4	5	4	7
USAF	20	-	-	-	-	-	-	-	-	4	5	4	7
US Navy.	3	1	-	-	1	1	-	-	-	-	-	-	-
Communications - Total	309	32	16	94	19	10	8	11	5	17	24	24	49
USAF	70	21	10	6	1	8	4	7	1	1	5	3	3
US Navy.	59	9	6	4	2	2	4	3	3	3	5	8	10
Army Field Forces.	177	-	-	84	16	-	-	1	1	13	14	13	35
National Guard Ground.	3	2	-	-	-	-	-	-	-	-	-	-	1
Special Research - Total	2	-	-	-	2	-	-	-	-	-	-	-	-
USAF	2	-	-	-	2	-	-	-	-	-	-	-	-

TABLE 15.-- FACTORY DELIVERIES OF ALL MILITARY JET PROPELLED AIRCRAFT ENGINES, BY PLANT, MODEL, AND UNIT POWER: 1948

Note: Unit Power is defined as pounds thrust and is shown after each model in parentheses. Excludes experimental models.

Plant, Model and Unit Power	1948
Total	2,443 a/
Allison: Indianapolis, Ind. - Total	1,753
J-33 (3750)	726
J-35 (4000)	1,027
General Electric: West Lynn, Mass. - Total	263
J-35 (4000) [Lockland Ohio]	18
J-47 (5000)	240
T-31 (1800)	5
Westinghouse: Philadelphia, Pa. - Total	427
J-30 (1600)	176
J-34 (3000)	251

a/ Acceptances for Dec 1948 for the Navy not available.

Source: Cost Control and Analysis Office, Comptroller's Department, Hq., Air Materiel Command.

TABLE 16.-- FACTORY DELIVERIES OF ALL MILITARY AIRCRAFT ENGINES, BY PLANT, BY MODEL, AND BY UNIT HORSEPOWER: 1948

Note: Unit horsepower is take-off horsepower. Excludes experimental, jet propelled, and engines manufactured for use in tanks.

Plant, Model and Horsepower	1948
Total	2,480 a/
Aircooled: Syracuse, N.Y. - Total	183
O-335 (175)	39
O-425 (250)	144
Allison: Indianapolis, Ind.	
V-1710 (1600)	145
Continental Motors: Muskegon, Mich.	
C-185E (185)	1
Pratt & Whitney: East Hartford, N.J. - Total	1,673
R-2000 (2000)	1
R-2800 (2300)	672
R-4360 (3000)	16
R-4360 (3500)	984
Wright: Patterson, N.J.	
R-3350 (2300)	478

a/ Acceptances for Dec 1948 for the Navy not available.

Source: Cost Control and Analysis Office, Comptroller's Department, Hq., Air Materiel Command.

TABLE 17.-- SUMMARY OF USAF AIRCRAFT ON HAND, BY MAJOR AIR COMMAND-INCLUDING AIR FORCE RESERVE, CIVIL AIR PATROL AND AIR NATIONAL GUARD-MONTHLY 1948

(Figures are as of end of month)

Command	January	February	March	April	May	June
Total	26,593	26,572	26,153	25,762	25,435	25,283
Continental US - Total	18,323	18,309	17,712	17,363	17,163	17,141
Air Defense Command a/	430	456	456	456	436	434
Air Materiel Command	12,625	12,417	12,405	12,088	11,859	11,614
Air Proving Ground Command b/	157	172	-	-	-	186
Air Training Command	1,659	1,754	1,379	1,457	1,549	1,546
Air University	343	344	341	306	293	277
Continental Air Command	-	-	-	-	-	-
Headquarters Command	179	166	170	172	162	168
Strategic Air Command	898	955	934	842	831	898
Tactical Air Command a/	1,261	1,276	1,334	1,339	1,337	1,338
Air Transport Service	771	769	694	703	696	680
Civil Air Patrol (Liaison)	-	-	-	-	-	-
Overseas - Total	4,870	4,826	4,643	4,518	4,381	4,256
Alaskan Air Command	231	256	254	259	277	280
Strategic Air Command (Overseas)	-	-	-	-	-	-
Caribbean Air Command	398	406	401	412	391	391
Far East Air Forces	2,057	2,168	2,161	2,155	2,205	2,096
Pacific Air Command	222	225	219	214	201	217
US Air Forces in Europe	1,836	1,666	1,516	1,284	1,159	1,115
Other Overseas c/	126	105	92	194	148	157
Reserve Forces - Total	3,400	3,437	3,797	3,881	3,891	3,886
Air Force Reserve	1,244	1,233	1,229	1,238	1,209	1,213
Civil Air Patrol	226	238	570	641	639	639
Air National Guard	1,930	1,966	1,998	2,002	2,043	2,034

a/ Air Defense Command and Tactical Air Command were discontinued as of 30 November 1948.
b/ Included with AMC January through May.
c/ Includes Army Advisory Group (China) and JBUSMC.

TABLE I 7 -- SUMMARY OF USAF AIRCRAFT ON HAND, BY MAJOR AIR COMMAND-INCLUDING AIR FORCE RESERVE, CIVIL AIR PATROL AND AIR NATIONAL GUARD-MONTHLY 1948 Continued

(Figures are as of end of month)

Command	July	August	September	October	November	December
Total	25,154	25,282	25,245	25,311	25,253	25,110
Continental US - Total	17,041	17,320	17,162	17,386	17,276	17,264
Air Defense Command	422	420	449	435	444	-
Air Materiel Command	11,485	11,595	11,565	11,515	11,336	11,107
Air Proving Ground Command	190	188	184	170	170	165
Air Training Command	1,525	1,527	1,534	1,640	1,745	1,820
Air University	284	286	287	286	281	287
Continental Air Command	-	-	-	-	-	1,974
Headquarters Command	172	179	206	207	208	205
Strategic Air Command	971	1,076	1,099	1,080	1,038	915
Tactical Air Command	1,317	1,376	1,348	1,339	1,347	-
Military Air Transport Service (Worldwide)	675	673	690	676	667	751
Civil Air Patrol (Liaison)	-	-	-	38	40	40
Overseas - Total	4,216	4,110	4,041	4,092	4,110	3,861
Alaskan Air Command	285	329	347	344	350	351
Strategic Air Command (Overseas)	137	113	116	-	-	-
Caribbean Air Command	288	289	285	296	295	274
Far East Air Forces	2,012	1,951	1,876	1,877	1,844	1,766
Pacific Air Command	202	197	193	182	178	170
US Air Forces in Europe	1,209	1,147	1,141	1,136	1,139	1,055
Other Overseas	83	84	83	257	304	245
Reserve Forces - Total	3,897	3,852	3,842	3,833	3,867	3,985
Air Force Reserve	1,210	1,210	1,221	1,200	1,213	1,250
Civil Air Patrol	639	597	592	586	585	587
Air National Guard	2,048	2,045	2,029	2,047	2,069	2,148

847201 O - 49 - 3

TABLE 18.— SUMMARY OF USAF AIRCRAFT ON HAND - INCLUDING AIR RESERVE FORCES AND CIVIL AIR PATROL BY COMMAND AND BY TYPE AND MODEL OF AIRCRAFT-AT END OF EACH QUARTER 1948

Type and Model	Total	Total Contl US (Incl ATC N/M)	ADC	AMC	AFTMC	AU	Hq Comd	SAC	TAC	ATC (N/M)
Continental										
31 March 1948	26,153	17,713	456	12,405	1,379	341	170	934	1,334	694
Bomber - Total	6,487	5,703	81	4,462	387	79	39	345	181	129
B-29	2,939	2,856	-	2,509	1	-	-	285	1	60
B-17	456	318	2	259	2	1	5	4	1	44
B-25	1,295	1,269	41	716	356	38	-	46	47	25
A-26	1,758	1,230	38	952	28	40	34	6	132	-
B-50	18	18	-	14	-	-	-	4	-	-
B-24	11	2	-	2	-	-	-	-	-	-
XB-26	1	1	-	1	-	-	-	-	-	-
XB-42	1	1	-	1	-	-	-	-	-	-
XB-43	1	1	-	1	-	-	-	-	-	-
XB-46	1	1	-	1	-	-	-	-	-	-
TA-20	1	1	-	1	-	-	-	-	-	-
RA-24	5	5	-	5	-	-	-	-	-	-
Fighter - Total	7,158	4,118	179	3,006	138	32	10	402	350	1
P-47	2,791	1,377	43	1,251	-	-	-	1	82	-
P-51	2,970	1,643	6	1,136	80	32	10	238	140	1
P-61	217	113	49	62	1	-	-	-	1	-
P-80	646	452	2	164	56	-	-	160	70	-
P-82	29	29	-	25	1	-	-	3	-	-
P-84	190	190	79	54	-	-	-	-	57	-
F8F	1	1	-	1	-	-	-	-	-	-
P-38	2	1	-	1	-	-	-	-	-	-
P-59	3	3	-	3	-	-	-	-	-	-
RP-63	307	307	-	307	-	-	-	-	-	-
XP-81	2	2	-	2	-	-	-	-	-	-
Reconnaissance - Total	651	423	-	217	8	-	-	44	136	18
F-2	51	34	-	24	5	-	-	5	-	-
F-6	142	92	-	51	-	-	-	-	40	1
F-9	73	25	-	4	-	-	-	21	-	-
F-13	92	73	-	60	-	-	-	13	-	-
FA-26	52	43	-	5	-	-	-	2	36	-
FP-80	136	100	-	40	-	-	-	-	60	-
F-15	31	7	-	7	-	-	-	-	-	-
RF-10	3	3	-	-	3	-	-	-	-	-
FL-17	1	1	-	-	-	-	-	1	-	-
OA-10	70	45	-	26	-	-	-	2	-	17
Transport - Total	3,640	2,296	150	913	146	108	108	95	300	477
C-45	646	407	72	129	4	91	49	12	20	30
C-47/53	1,762	1,147	78	450	137	17	48	71	121	225
C-54	463	356	-	142	2	-	-	12	12	188
C-74	12	12	-	5	-	-	-	-	-	7
C-82	169	169	-	14	2	-	-	-	143	10
C-117	14	12	-	1	-	-	11	-	-	-
C-97	7	7	-	5	-	-	-	-	-	2
C-64	60	8	-	1	-	-	-	-	-	7
C-46	476	160	-	151	1	-	-	-	-	8
C-118	1	1	-	1	-	-	-	-	-	-
C-3	20	11	-	8	-	-	-	-	3	-
OA-12	4	4	-	4	-	-	-	-	-	-
OA-9	2	1	-	1	-	-	-	-	-	-
XC-113	1	1	-	-	-	-	-	-	1	-
C-78	3	-	-	-	-	-	-	-	-	-
Trainer - Total	5,774	3,643	44	2,719	604	113	12	46	99	6
AT-6	3,504	2,062	43	1,205	520	75	12	46	98	3
AT-7/AT-11	1,245	902	-	860	-	38	-	-	1	3
PT-13	830	491	1	406	84	-	-	-	-	-
BT-13	66	62	-	62	-	-	-	-	-	-
PT-17	17	14	-	14	-	-	-	-	-	-
PT-19	112	112	-	112	-	-	-	-	-	-
Communications - Total	1,531	813	2	540	96	9	1	2	100	63
Liaison	1,408	729	2	512	64	9	1	2	93	46
Rotary Wing	123	84	-	28	32	-	-	-	7	17
Gliders and Targets	912	717	-	549	-	-	-	-	168	-

TABLE 18.-- SUMMARY OF USAF AIRCRAFT ON HAND - INCLUDING AIR RESERVE FORCES AND CIVIL AIR PATROL BY COMMAND AND BY TYPE AND MODEL OF AIRCRAFT: AT END OF EACH QUARTER 1948-- Continued

Type and Model	Total Overseas (Excl ATC W/h)	AAC	CairC	FEAF	PAC	USAFE	Misc. Overseas a/	Reserve Forces and CAP			
								Total	AF Reserve	CAP	ANG
				Overseas								
31 March 1948	4,643	254	401	2,161	219	1,516	92	2,797	1,229	570	1,998
Bomber - Total	433	21	51	229	22	92	17	351	-	-	351
B-29	83	5	-	62	2	1	13	-	-	-	-
B-17	138	10	30	56	7	34	1	-	-	-	-
B-25	26	2	11	9	1	-	3	-	-	-	-
A-26	177	4	10	102	4	57	-	351	-	-	351
B-24	9	-	-	-	-	9	-	-	-	-	-
Fighter - Total	1,850	107	95	869	118	661	-	1,190	-	-	1,190
P-47	955	-	-	292	117	546	-	459	-	-	459
P-51	596	69	-	412	-	115	-	731	-	-	731
F-61	104	10	12	82	-	-	-	-	-	-	-
P-80	194	28	83	83	-	-	-	-	-	-	-
P-82	-	-	-	-	-	-	-	-	-	-	-
F-84	-	-	-	-	-	-	-	-	-	-	-
F-38	1	-	-	-	1	-	-	-	-	-	-
Reconnaissance - Total	228	10	50	142	1	21	4	-	-	-	-
F-2	17	-	3	13	-	-	1	-	-	-	-
F-6	50	-	-	39	-	11	-	-	-	-	-
F-9	48	-	17	29	-	2	-	-	-	-	-
F-13	19	7	-	10	-	-	2	-	-	-	-
FA-26	9	-	-	1	-	8	-	-	-	-	-
FP-80	36	-	18	18	-	-	-	-	-	-	-
F-15	24	-	-	24	-	-	-	-	-	-	-
OA-10	25	3	12	8	1	-	1	-	-	-	-
Transport - Total	1,216	65	120	409	39	534	49	128	-	9	119
C-45	229	7	25	19	3	171	4	10	-	8	2
C-47/53	500	37	69	40	2	310	42	115	-	1	114
C-54	107	14	22	47	19	2	3	-	-	-	-
C-74	-	-	-	-	-	-	-	-	-	-	-
C-82	-	-	-	-	-	-	-	-	-	-	-
C-117	2	-	-	-	-	2	-	-	-	-	-
C-46	313	1	-	299	13	-	-	3	-	-	3
C-64	52	6	-	-	-	46	-	-	-	-	-
CQ-3	9	-	3	4	2	-	-	-	-	-	-
OA-9	1	-	1	-	-	-	-	-	-	-	-
C-78	3	-	-	-	-	3	-	-	-	-	-
Trainer - Total	271	15	21	173	17	25	20	1,860	1,229	362	269
AT-6	242	5	17	173	17	24	6	1,200	934	34	232
AT-7/AT-11	11	10	-	-	-	1	-	332	295	-	37
BT-13	4	-	4	-	-	-	-	-	-	-	-
JT-17	-	-	-	-	-	-	-	3	-	3	-
PT-13	14	-	-	-	-	-	14	325	-	325	-
Communications - Total	450	26	32	198	9	183	2	268	-	199	69
Liaison	411	15	27	177	7	183	2	268	-	199	69
Rotary Wing	39	11	5	21	2	-	-	-	-	-	-
Gliders and Targets	195	10	32	141	12	-	-	-	-	-	-

a/ Includes JBUSMC, AAG, and Enroute

TABLE 18.-- SUMMARY OF USAF AIRCRAFT ON HAND.- INCLUDING AIR, RESERVE FORCES AND CIVIL AIR PATROL BY COMMAND AND BY TYPE AND MODEL OF AIRCRAFT: AT END OF EACH QUARTER 1948 -- Continued

Type and Model	Total	Total Contl US (Incl ATC n/h)	ADC	AMC	AFG	AFTHC	AU	Hq Comd	SAC	TAC	ATC (n/h)
				Continental							
30 June 1948	25,283	17,141	434	11,614	186	1,546	277	168	898	1,328	680
Bomber - Total	6,191	5,434	106	4,033	97	377	73	41	371	187	129
B-29	2,735	2,641	-	2,247	19	1	-	-	314	1	59
B-17	372	239	2	147	32	2	-	6	5	1	44
B-25	1,319	1,305	54	704	16	347	39	35	45	42	23
A-26	1,712	1,185	50	897	27	27	34	-	4	143	3
B-50	26	26	-	22	2	-	-	-	2	-	-
B-36	4	4	-	2	1	-	-	-	1	-	-
B-24	11	2	-	2	-	-	-	-	-	-	-
B-42	1	1	-	1	-	-	-	-	-	-	-
B-43	2	2	-	2	-	-	-	-	-	-	-
B-45	3	3	-	3	-	-	-	-	-	-	-
B-46	1	1	-	1	-	-	-	-	-	-	-
A-24	5	5	-	5	-	-	-	-	-	-	-
Fighter - Total	6,823	4,022	166	2,943	38	164	30	10	240	331	-
P-47	2,427	1,318	25	1,211	4	1	-	-	-	77	-
P-51	2,887	1,541	9	1,121	4	104	30	10	167	96	-
P-61	205	103	45	54	2	2	-	-	-	-	-
P-80	653	410	1	156	11	56	-	-	112	74	-
P-82	60	60	1	21	8	-	-	-	30	-	-
P-84	275	275	85	67	7	1	-	-	31	84	-
F-87	1	1	-	-	1	-	-	-	-	-	-
P-59	2	2	-	2	-	-	-	-	-	-	-
P-63	307	307	-	307	-	-	-	-	-	-	-
P-81	2	2	-	2	-	-	-	-	-	-	-
P-86	2	2	-	2	-	-	-	-	-	-	-
P-38	2	1	-	-	1	-	-	-	-	-	-
Reconnaissance - Total	640	410	-	190	10	9	-	-	43	139	19
F-2	51	33	-	23	-	5	-	-	5	-	-
F-6	141	91	-	48	-	-	-	-	-	42	1
F-9	74	26	-	4	-	-	-	-	22	-	-
F-13	87	67	-	51	2	-	-	-	14	-	-
FA-26	51	43	-	5	-	-	-	-	-	38	-
FP-80	135	100	-	32	8	1	-	-	-	59	-
F-10	3	3	-	-	-	3	-	-	-	-	-
F-11	1	1	-	1	-	-	-	-	-	-	-
F-15	31	4	-	4	-	-	-	-	-	-	-
OA-10	66	42	-	22	-	-	-	-	2	-	18
Supersonic Test	2	2	-	2	-	-	-	-	-	-	-
Transport - Total	3,576	2,332	148	896	25	146	124	111	98	321	463
C-45	600	398	70	97	8	4	103	52	13	20	31
C-47/53	1,720	1,132	78	412	15	140	21	48	73	123	222
C-54	462	349	-	141	1	-	-	-	11	12	184
C-74	12	12	-	7	1	-	-	-	-	-	4
C-82	186	182	-	13	-	2	-	-	1	162	4
C-117	14	12	-	1	-	-	-	11	-	-	-
C-97	8	8	-	5	-	-	-	-	-	-	3
C-118	1	1	-	-	-	-	-	-	-	-	1
CG-3	24	17	-	14	-	-	-	-	-	3	-
C-46	492	209	-	202	-	-	-	-	-	-	7
C-60	1	-	-	-	-	-	-	-	-	-	-
C-112	1	1	-	1	-	-	-	-	-	-	-
C-113	1	1	-	1	-	-	-	-	-	1	-
C-119	1	1	-	1	-	-	-	-	-	-	-
OA-9	2	1	-	1	-	-	-	-	-	-	-
OA-12	3	-	-	-	-	-	-	-	-	-	-
C-64	48	8	-	1	-	-	-	-	-	-	7
Trainer - Total	5,625	3,469	12	2,523	10	737	41	6	43	95	6
AT-6	3,472	2,069	11	1,167	10	734	4	4	43	93	3
AT-7/AT-11	1,108	762	-	717	-	3	37	-	-	2	3
BT-13	65	62	-	62	-	-	-	-	-	-	-
IT-13	793	406	1	405	-	-	-	-	-	-	-
PT-17	31	14	-	14	-	-	-	-	-	-	-
PT-19	112	112	-	112	-	-	-	-	-	-	-
SNJ-4	44	44	-	44	-	-	-	-	-	-	-
Communications - Total	1,552	814	2	504	6	113	9	2	3	112	63
Liaison	1,413	719	2	480	4	74	9	2	3	102	43
Rotary Wing	139	95	-	24	2	39	-	-	-	10	20
Gliders and Targets	874	678	-	525	-	-	-	-	-	153	-

TABLE 18.-- SUMMARY OF USAF AIRCRAFT ON HAND - INCLUDING AIR RESERVE FORCES AND CIVIL AIR PATROL BY COMMAND AND BY TYPE AND MODEL OF AIRCRAFT: AT END OF EACH QUARTER 1948 -- Continued

Type and Model	Total Overseas (Excl. ATC W/W)	AAC	CairC	FEAF	PAC	USAF	Misc. Overseas a/	Reserve Forces and CAP Total	AF Reserve	CAP	ANG
Overseas
30 June 1948	4,256	280	391	2,096	217	1,115	157	3,886	1,213	639	2,034
Bomber - Total	421	22	39	221	22	85	32	356	8	-	348
B-29	94	4	-	60	1	1	28	-	-	-	-
B-17	133	12	27	53	7	33	1	-	-	-	-
B-25	14	2	1	7	1	-	3	-	-	-	-
A-26	171	4	11	101	4	51	-	356	8	-	348
B-24	9	-	-	-	9	-	-	-	-	-	-
Fighter - Total	1,564	118	94	843	101	349	59	1,237	-	-	1,237
P-47	606	-	-	227	100	279	-	503	-	-	503
P-51	622	80	-	413	-	70	59	724	-	-	724
P-61	102	10	12	80	-	-	-	-	-	-	-
P-80	233	28	82	123	-	-	-	10	-	-	10
P-82	-	-	-	-	-	-	-	-	-	-	-
P-84	-	-	-	-	-	-	-	-	-	-	-
P-38	1	-	-	-	1	-	-	-	-	-	-
Reconnaissance - Total	230	14	48	146	-	21	1	-	-	-	-
F-2	18	1	3	13	-	-	1	-	-	-	-
F-6	50	-	-	39	-	11	-	-	-	-	-
F-9	48	-	17	29	-	2	-	-	-	-	-
F-13	20	8	-	12	-	-	-	-	-	-	-
FA-26	8	-	-	-	-	8	-	-	-	-	-
FP-80	35	-	17	18	-	-	-	-	-	-	-
F-15	27	-	-	27	-	-	-	-	-	-	-
OA-10	24	5	11	8	-	-	-	-	-	-	-
Transport - Total	1,117	77	126	381	47	442	44	127	-	10	117
C-45	191	7	25	19	8	132	-	11	-	9	2
C-47/53	474	45	72	41	4	271	41	114	-	1	113
C-54	113	13	24	57	15	2	2	-	-	-	-
C-74	-	-	-	-	-	-	-	-	-	-	-
C-82	4	3	-	-	-	-	1	-	-	-	-
C-117	2	-	-	-	-	2	-	-	-	-	-
C-3	7	-	3	2	2	-	-	-	-	-	-
C-46	281	1	-	262	18	-	-	2	-	-	2
C-60	1	-	1	-	-	-	-	-	-	-	-
OA-9	1	-	1	-	-	-	-	-	-	-	-
CA-12	3	3	-	-	-	-	-	-	-	-	-
C-64	40	5	-	-	-	35	-	-	-	-	-
Trainer - Total	265	15	19	172	16	24	19	1,891	1,205	419	267
AT-6	238	5	16	172	16	24	5	1,165	906	29	230
AT-7/AT-11	10	10	-	-	-	-	-	336	299	-	37
BT-13	3	-	3	-	-	-	-	-	-	-	-
PT-17	14	-	-	-	-	-	14	3	-	3	-
PT-13	-	-	-	-	-	-	-	387	-	387	-
Communications - Total	463	25	37	183	22	194	2	275	-	210	65
Liaison	419	15	27	161	20	194	2	275	-	210	65
Rotary Wing	44	10	10	22	2	-	-	-	-	-	-
Gliders and Targets	196	9	28	150	9	-	-	-	-	-	-

a/ Includes JBUSMC and AAC

TABLE 18.— SUMMARY OF USAF AIRCRAFT ON HAND — INCLUDING AIR RESERVE FORCES AND CIVIL AIR PATROL BY COMMAND AND BY TYPE AND MODEL OF AIRCRAFT: AT END OF EACH QUARTER 1948 — Continued

Type and Model	Total	Total Contl US (Incl MATS W/N)	ADC	AMC	AFG	AFTRC	AU	Hq Comd	SAC	TAC	MATS (N/ii)
Continental											
30 September 1948	25,245	17,362	449	11,565	184	1,534	287	206	1,099	1,348	690
Bomber - Total	4,153	3,487	28	2,967	52	2	19	2	320	81	16
B-29	2,021	1,847	-	1,534	9	-	1	-	297	1	5
B-50	48	48	-	43	2	-	-	-	3	-	-
B-17	169	127	-	97	23	-	-	1	-	-	6
B-26	1,375	937	28	789	14	1	18	1	3	80	3
B-36	20	20	-	3	1	-	-	-	16	-	-
B-35	1	1	-	1	-	-	-	-	-	-	-
B-24	6	2	-	2	-	-	-	-	-	-	-
B-25	495	487	-	483	-	1	-	-	1	-	2
B-42	1	1	-	1	-	-	-	-	-	-	-
B-43	2	2	-	2	-	-	-	-	-	-	-
B-45	14	14	-	11	3	-	-	-	-	-	-
B-46	1	1	-	1	-	-	-	-	-	-	-
Fighter - Total	5,753	3,187	174	2,060	40	25	10	-	522	353	3
F-47	1,861	873	10	785	3	1	-	-	-	73	1
F-51	2,552	1,384	3	1,057	6	17	9	-	206	86	-
F-61	159	70	45	21	1	1	-	-	-	-	2
F-80	671	350	2	105	11	5	-	-	155	72	-
F-82	145	145	29	28	5	1	-	-	82	-	-
F-84	348	348	85	49	12	-	1	-	79	122	-
F-8	1	1	-	-	1	-	-	-	-	-	-
F-24	5	5	-	5	-	-	-	-	-	-	-
F-38	1	1	-	1	-	-	-	-	-	-	-
F-59	2	2	-	2	-	-	-	-	-	-	-
F-81	2	2	-	2	-	-	-	-	-	-	-
F-86	6	6	-	5	1	-	-	-	-	-	-
Reconnaissance - Total	603	391	-	153	9	9	-	1	46	117	56
RB-17	77	29	-	4	-	-	-	-	20	-	5
RB-29	137	118	-	44	2	-	-	-	21	-	51
RB-26	59	43	-	5	-	-	-	1	-	37	-
RF-51	112	65	-	43	-	-	-	-	-	22	-
RF-80	132	99	-	34	7	-	-	-	-	58	-
RC-45	51	28	-	17	-	6	-	-	5	-	-
R-11	1	1	-	1	-	-	-	-	-	-	-
R-12	1	1	-	1	-	-	-	-	-	-	-
RB-25	3	3	-	-	-	3	-	-	-	-	-
RF-61	30	4	-	4	-	-	-	-	-	-	-
Search and Rescue	99	42	-	4	-	-	-	-	-	-	38
Combat Amphibian	41	21	-	14	-	-	-	-	1	-	6
Special Research	2	2	-	2	-	-	-	-	-	-	-
Transport - Total	3,820	2,602	154	1,153	25	97	141	155	114	288	475
C-45	615	418	71	97	8	4	117	65	12	17	27
C-47/C-117	1,618	1,046	76	392	16	77	20	66	78	111	210
C-54	459	349	-	128	1	-	-	-	11	1	208
C-82	205	167	2	14	-	-	-	-	-	146	5
CB-17	9	2	-	-	-	-	-	-	1	-	1
CB-25	55	55	-	28	-	2	1	15	-	9	-
CB-26	4	4	1	1	-	-	1	1	-	-	-
C-74	12	12	-	8	-	-	-	-	-	-	4
C-97	8	8	-	7	-	-	-	-	1	-	-
C-112	1	1	-	1	-	-	-	-	-	-	-

TABLE 18.- SUMMARY OF USAF AIRCRAFT ON HAND - INCLUDING AIR RESERVE FORCES AND CIVIL AIR PATROL BY COMMAND AND BY TYPE AND MODEL OF AIRCRAFT: AT END OF EACH QUARTER 1948 -- Continued

Type and Model	Total	Total Contl US (Incl MATS W/W)	ADC	AMC	APG	AFTRC	AU	Hq.Comd	SAC	TAC	MATS (W/W)
30 September 1948 (Contd)				Continental (Continued)							
Transport - Total (Contd)											
C-119	1	1	-	1	-	-	-	-	-	-	-
C-46	696	461	-	453	-	-	-	-	-	-	8
C-53	9	-	-	-	-	-	-	-	-	-	-
C-113	1	1	-	-	-	-	-	-	-	-	-
VB-17	25	15	1	5	-	1	-	-	-	1	2
VB-25	34	34	1	9	-	7	1	4	1	-	2
VB-26	16	16	2	5	-	6	-	4	10	-	2
C-118	1	1	-	-	-	-	-	-	-	3	-
C-64	42	7	-	-	-	-	-	-	-	-	1
A-9	2	1	-	1	-	-	-	-	-	-	7
A-12	6	3	-	3	-	-	-	-	-	-	-
CB-24	1	-	-	-	-	-	-	-	-	-	-
Trainer - Total	8,202	5,888	90	3,921	53	1,305	108	47	94	237	24
T-6	3,518	2,134	13	1,183	7	747	4	4	45	128	3
T-7/T-11	1,099	761	-	716	-	5	35	-	1	1	3
TB-17	70	46	1	28	6	1	-	1	2	1	6
TB-25	729	724	49	171	15	339	35	35	36	25	19
TB-26	300	223	17	100	13	21	12	-	3	57	-
TB-29	605	605	-	588	11	-	-	-	5	-	1
TC-47	89	89	-	25	-	63	-	-	-	-	1
TF-51	286	207	9	81	-	81	22	7	2	5	-
TF-80	52	52	-	5	-	47	-	-	-	-	-
SNJ-4	1	1	-	1	-	-	-	-	-	-	-
TRB-29	2	2	-	2	-	-	-	-	-	-	-
TF-47	438	421	-	418	-	-	-	-	-	3	-
TRF-51	24	24	-	5	-	1	-	-	-	17	1
TR-61	5	5	-	5	-	-	-	-	-	-	-
BT-13	65	62	-	62	-	-	-	-	-	-	-
PT-13	793	406	1	405	-	-	-	-	-	-	-
T-17	14	14	-	14	-	-	-	-	-	-	-
T-19	112	112	-	112	-	-	-	-	-	-	-
Communications - Total	1,415	772	3	471	6	96	9	1	2	122	62
Liaison	1,278	669	3	437	4	59	9	1	2	112	42
Rotary Wing	137	103	-	34	2	37	-	-	-	10	20
Gliders and Targets	1,157	970	-	820	-	-	-	-	-	150	-

TABLE 18.-- SUMMARY OF USAF AIRCRAFT ON HAND - INCLUDING AIR RESERVE FORCES AND CIVIL AIR PATROL BY COMMAND AND BY TYPE AND MODEL OF AIRCRAFT: AT END OF EACH QUARTER 1948 -- Continued

Type and Model	Total Overseas (Excl MATS n/a)	AAC	CairC	FEAF	PAC	USAFE	Misc. Overseas a/	Reserve Forces and CAP Total	AF Reserve	CAP	ANG
Overseas											
30 September 1948	4,041	347	285	1,876	193	1,141	199	3,843	1,221	592	2,029
Bomber - Total	375	16	1	161	5	71	119	291	10	-	281
B-29	174	4	-	53	1	1	115	-	-	-	-
B-50	-	-	-	-	-	-	-	-	-	-	-
B-17	42	8	-	4	-	29	1	-	-	-	-
B-26	147	4	3	99	-	41	-	291	10	-	281
B-24	4	-	-	-	4	-	-	-	-	-	-
B-25	8	-	-	5	-	-	3	-	-	-	-
Fighter - Total	1,421	185	12	735	96	388	5	1,145	-	-	1,145
F-47	504	-	-	165	96	243	-	484	-	-	484
F-51	536	82	-	389	-	65	-	632	-	-	632
F-61	89	9	12	68	-	-	-	-	-	-	-
F-80	292	94	-	113	-	80	5	29	-	-	29
F-82	-	-	-	-	-	-	-	-	-	-	-
F-84	-	-	-	-	-	-	-	-	-	-	-
Reconnaissance - Total	212	8	35	142	-	25	2	-	-	-	-
RB-17	48	-	17	29	-	1	1	-	-	-	-
RB-29	19	7	-	12	-	-	-	-	-	-	-
RB-26	16	-	-	-	-	16	-	-	-	-	-
RF-51	47	-	-	39	-	8	-	-	-	-	-
RF-80	33	-	15	18	-	-	-	-	-	-	-
RC-45	23	1	3	18	-	-	1	-	-	-	-
RF-61	26	-	-	26	-	-	-	-	-	-	-
Search and Rescue	57	-	9	34	12	2	-	-	-	-	-
Combat Amphibian	20	6	7	7	-	-	-	-	-	-	-
Special Research	-	-	-	-	-	-	-	-	-	-	-
Transport - Total	1,097	76	113	339	42	463	64	121	1	1	119
C-45	194	7	28	19	12	128	-	3	1	-	2
C-47/C-117	457	44	69	39	5	267	33	115	-	1	114
C-54	110	11	11	56	5	25	2	-	-	-	-
C-82	38	4	-	-	-	5	29	-	-	-	-
CB-17	7	1	3	1	2	-	-	-	-	-	-
CB-25	-	-	-	-	-	-	-	-	-	-	-
CB-26	-	-	-	-	-	-	-	-	-	-	-
C-46	233	1	-	215	17	-	-	2	-	-	2
C-53	8	-	-	-	-	8	-	1	-	-	1
VB-17	10	-	1	9	-	-	-	-	-	-	-
CB-24	1	-	-	-	1	-	-	-	-	-	-
C-64	35	5	-	-	-	30	-	-	-	-	-
A-9	1	-	1	-	-	-	-	-	-	-	-
A-12	3	3	-	-	-	-	-	-	-	-	-
Trainer - Total	290	21	48	173	18	24	6	2,024	1,210	387	427
T-6	235	5	16	171	14	24	5	1,149	917	-	232
T/7-T/11	11	11	-	-	-	-	-	327	292	-	35
TB-17	24	3	20	-	-	-	1	-	-	-	-
TB-25	5	2	1	2	-	-	-	-	-	-	-
TB-26	12	-	8	-	4	-	-	65	1	-	64
TB-29	-	-	-	-	-	-	-	-	-	-	-
TC-47	-	-	-	-	-	-	-	-	-	-	-
TF-51	-	-	-	-	-	-	-	79	-	-	79
TF-80	-	-	-	-	-	-	-	-	-	-	-
TF-47	-	-	-	-	-	-	-	17	-	-	17
BT-13	3	-	3	-	-	-	-	-	-	-	-
PT-13	-	-	-	-	-	-	-	387	-	387	-
Communications - Total	382	24	33	143	11	168	3	261	-	204	57
Liaison	348	14	24	128	11	168	3	261	-	204	57
Rotary Wing	34	10	9	15	-	-	-	-	-	-	-
Gliders and Targets	187	11	25	142	9	-	-	-	-	-	-

a/ Includes JHUSMC and AAC

TABLE 18.-- SUMMARY OF USAF AIRCRAFT ON HAND - INCLUDING AIR RESERVE FORCES AND CIVIL AIR PATROL BY COMMAND AND BY TYPE AND MODEL OF AIRCRAFT: AT END OF EACH QUARTER 1948 -- Continued

Type and Model	Total	Total Contl US (Incl MATS n/h)	AMC	APG	AFTRC	AU	ConAC	Hq Comd	SAC	CAP (Liaison)	MATS (t/h)
Continental											
31 December 1948	25,110	17,264	11,107	165	1,820	287	1,974	205	915	40	751
Bomber - Total	4,189	3,529	2,844	45	53	19	105	2	441	-	20
B-36	39	39	7	2	-	-	-	-	30	-	-
B-29	2,058	1,907	1,510	11	-	-	2	-	376	-	8
B-35	2	2	2	-	-	-	-	-	-	-	-
B-47	1	1	1	-	-	-	-	-	-	-	-
B-48	2	2	2	-	-	-	-	-	-	-	-
B-50	73	70	40	2	-	-	-	-	28	-	-
B-17	155	116	93	15	1	-	-	1	-	-	6
B-24	2	2	2	-	-	-	-	-	-	-	-
B-25	475	467	411	-	51	-	-	-	2	-	3
B-26	1,356	897	753	12	1	19	103	1	5	-	3
B-26H	1	1	1	-	-	-	-	-	-	-	-
B-42	1	1	1	-	-	-	-	-	-	-	-
B-43	2	2	2	-	-	-	-	-	-	-	-
B-45	21	21	18	3	-	-	-	-	-	-	-
B-46	1	1	1	-	-	-	-	-	-	-	-
Fighter - Total	5,697	3,056	2,016	41	34	10	724	4	226	-	1
F-24	5	5	5	-	-	-	-	-	-	-	-
F-47	1,790	831	747	2	-	-	82	-	-	-	-
F-51	2,415	1,217	977	7	28	10	69	4	122	-	-
F-61	116	43	27	1	-	-	13	-	1	-	1
F-80	722	329	108	16	5	-	186	-	14	-	-
F-81	2	2	2	-	-	-	-	-	-	-	-
F-82	242	225	73	5	1	-	65	-	81	-	-
F-84	394	393	68	8	-	-	309	-	8	-	-
F-86	10	10	8	2	-	-	-	-	-	-	-
F-87	1	1	1	-	-	-	-	-	-	-	-
Reconnaissance - Total	588	386	147	9	9	-	110	1	56	1	53
R-11	1	1	-	1	-	-	-	-	-	-	-
R-12	1	1	1	-	-	-	-	-	-	-	-
RB-17	74	28	2	-	-	-	-	-	23	-	3
RB-25	3	3	-	-	3	-	-	-	-	-	-
RB-29	139	119	40	-	-	-	-	-	29	-	50
RB-26	59	43	5	-	-	-	37	1	-	-	-
RC-45	50	27	17	-	6	-	-	-	3	1	-
RF-51	104	65	43	1	-	-	21	-	-	-	-
RC-54	1	1	-	-	-	-	-	-	1	-	-
RF-61	29	4	4	-	-	-	-	-	-	-	-
RF-80	127	94	35	7	-	-	52	-	-	-	-
Search and Rescue-Total	99	50	13	-	-	-	-	-	-	-	37
SL-5	6	-	-	-	-	-	-	-	-	-	-
SH-5	1	-	-	-	-	-	-	-	-	-	-
SH-6	2	-	-	-	-	-	-	-	-	-	-
SA-10	18	17	-	-	-	-	-	-	-	-	17
SB-17	70	33	13	-	-	-	-	-	-	-	20
SC-46	1	-	-	-	-	-	-	-	-	-	-
SC-47	1	-	-	-	-	-	-	-	-	-	-
Combat - Amphibian	42	22	17	-	-	-	-	-	1	-	4
A-10	41	22	17	-	-	-	-	-	1	-	4
PBY-5	1	-	-	-	-	-	-	-	-	-	-
Special Research -Total	2	2	2	-	-	-	-	-	-	-	-
X-1	2	2	2	-	-	-	-	-	-	-	-

TABLE 1B.-- SUMMARY OF USAF AIRCRAFT ON HAND- INCLUDING AIR RESERVE FORCES AND CIVIL AIR PATROL BY COMMAND AND BY TYPE AND MODEL OF AIRCRAFT: AT END OF EACH QUARTER 1948 -- Continued

Type and Model	Total	Total Contl US (Incl MATS o/s)	CAC	APG	AFTRC	AU	ConAC	Hq Cond	SAC	CAP-(Liaison)	MATS (o/s)
31 December 1948 (Contd)					Continental (Continued)						
Transport - Total	2,837	2,683	1,162	24	108	143	426	152	108	10	540
C-74	12	12	3	-	-	-	-	-	-	-	9
C-97	9	9	4	-	-	-	-	-	3	-	2
C-54	453	425	130	-	1	-	-	-	10	-	284
C-112	1	1	1	-	-	-	-	-	-	-	-
C-119	1	1	1	-	-	-	-	-	-	-	-
C-121	2	2	1	-	-	-	-	-	-	-	1
C-46	687	450	444	-	-	-	-	-	-	-	6
C-47	1,623	1,027	409	15	73	21	188	56	72	1	192
C-53	9	-	-	-	-	-	-	-	-	-	-
C-82	204	185	19	1	-	1	152	-	1	-	11
CB-17	8	2	1	-	-	1	-	-	-	-	-
VB-17	33	19	9	-	2	-	1	2	2	-	1
CB-25	54	54	27	-	4	1	8	14	-	-	-
VB-25	40	40	12	-	11	1	2	4	9	-	1
CB-26	4	4	1	-	-	1	1	1	-	-	-
VB-26	19	19	8	-	6	-	5	-	-	-	-
C-118	1	1	-	-	-	-	-	-	-	-	1
C-45	591	397	75	8	11	117	77	63	11	9	26
DC-45	24	17	15	-	-	-	2	-	-	-	-
C-64	42	6	-	-	-	-	-	-	-	-	6
C-117	15	11	1	-	-	-	-	10	-	-	-
A-9	2	1	1	-	-	-	-	-	-	-	-
A-12	3	-	-	-	-	-	-	-	-	-	-
Trainer - Total	8,196	5,889	2,733	32	1,515	106	319	45	76	28	32
T-6	3,502	2,137	1,044	3	902	4	128	4	21	23	3
T-7	437	415	377	-	-	34	1	-	-	-	1
T-11	659	339	332	-	4	-	-	-	1	-	2
TB-17	66	39	26	4	-	-	2	1	1	-	5
TB-25	738	734	149	4	385	34	75	33	36	-	18
TB-26	311	225	98	12	20	12	80	-	3	-	-
TB-29	555	555	539	11	-	-	-	-	4	-	2
TRB-29	1	1	-	-	-	-	-	-	1	-	-
TC-47	88	88	24	-	63	-	-	-	-	-	1
TF-47	435	420	417	-	-	-	3	-	-	-	-
TF-51	290	214	81	-	82	22	13	7	9	-	-
TRF-51	22	22	5	-	-	-	15	-	-	-	1
TF-61	2	2	2	-	-	-	-	-	-	-	-
TF-80	65	65	5	1	59	-	-	-	-	-	-
BT-13	65	62	62	-	-	-	-	-	-	-	-
TT-13	834	447	446	-	-	-	1	-	-	-	-
T-17	14	14	14	-	-	-	-	-	-	-	-
T-19	112	112	112	-	-	-	-	-	-	-	-
Communication - Total	1,403	765	455	7	101	9	122	1	7	1	61
L-4	468	245	182	1	29	-	26	-	4	-	3
L-5	664	293	219	2	10	1	34	1	1	1	24
L-13	105	103	24	2	1	8	51	-	2	-	15
L-15	2	2	2	-	-	-	-	-	-	-	-
L-16	21	21	1	-	20	-	-	-	-	-	-
L-17	3	1	1	-	-	-	-	-	-	-	-
H-4	1	1	1	-	-	-	-	-	-	-	-
H-5	81	53	11	2	9	-	12	-	-	-	19
H-6	42	30	7	-	25	-	-	-	-	-	-
H-9	1	1	1	-	-	-	-	-	-	-	-
H-10	1	1	1	-	-	-	-	-	-	-	-
H-12	1	1	1	-	-	-	-	-	-	-	-
H-13	13	13	4	-	9	-	-	-	-	-	-
Gliders and Targets	1,057	882	718	4	-	-	157	-	-	-	2

TABLE 18.-- SUMMARY OF USAF AIRCRAFT ON HAND - INCLUDING AIR RESERVE FORCES AND CIVIL AIR PATROL BY COMMAND AND BY TYPE AND MODEL OF AIRCRAFT: AT END OF EACH QUARTER 1948 -- Continued

Type and Model	Total Overseas (Excl MAIS(N/N)	AAC	CairC	FEAF	PAC	USAFE	Misc. Overseas a/	Reserve Forces and CAP Total	Reserve	CAP	ANG
				Overseas							
31 December 1948	3,861	351	274	1,766	170	1,055	245	3,985	1,250	587	2,148
Bomber - Total	346	19	3	156	1	67	100	314	42	-	272
B-36	-	-	-	-	-	-	-	-	-	-	-
B-29	151	5	-	50	1	1	94	-	-	-	-
B-35	-	-	-	-	-	-	-	-	-	-	-
B-47	-	-	-	-	-	-	-	-	-	-	-
B-48	-	-	-	-	-	-	-	-	-	-	-
B-50	3	2	-	-	-	-	1	-	-	-	-
B-17	39	8	-	4	-	25	2	-	-	-	-
B-24	-	-	-	-	-	-	-	-	-	-	-
B-25	8	-	-	5	-	-	3	-	-	-	-
B-26	145	4	3	97	-	41	-	314	42	-	272
B-26B	-	-	-	-	-	-	-	-	-	-	-
B-42	-	-	-	-	-	-	-	-	-	-	-
B-43	-	-	-	-	-	-	-	-	-	-	-
B-45	-	-	-	-	-	-	-	-	-	-	-
B-46	-	-	-	-	-	-	-	-	-	-	-
Fighter - Total	1,369	190	15	704	93	346	21	1,272	-	-	1,272
F-24	-	-	-	-	-	-	-	-	-	-	-
F-47	478	1	-	142	93	242	-	481	-	-	481
F-51	496	82	-	388	-	26	-	702	-	-	702
P-61	73	9	-	64	-	-	-	-	-	-	-
F-80	304	95	-	110	-	78	21	89	-	-	89
F-81	-	-	-	-	-	-	-	-	-	-	-
F-82	17	2	15	-	-	-	-	-	-	-	-
F-84	1	1	-	-	-	-	-	-	-	-	-
F-86	-	-	-	-	-	-	-	-	-	-	-
F-87	-	-	-	-	-	-	-	-	-	-	-
Reconnaissance - Total	202	8	35	137	-	20	2	-	-	-	-
R-11	-	-	-	-	-	-	-	-	-	-	-
R-12	-	-	-	-	-	-	-	-	-	-	-
RB-17	46	-	17	28	-	1	-	-	-	-	-
RB-25	-	-	-	-	-	-	-	-	-	-	-
RB-26	16	-	-	-	-	16	-	-	-	-	-
RB-29	20	7	-	12	-	-	1	-	-	-	-
RC-45	23	1	3	18	-	-	1	-	-	-	-
RF-51	39	-	-	36	-	3	-	-	-	-	-
RC-54	-	-	-	-	-	-	-	-	-	-	-
RF-61	25	-	-	25	-	-	-	-	-	-	-
RF-80	33	-	15	18	-	-	-	-	-	-	-
Search and Rescue	49	-	4	30	12	3	-	-	-	-	-
SL-5	6	-	2	-	4	-	-	-	-	-	-
SH-5	1	-	1	-	-	-	-	-	-	-	-
SH-6	2	-	-	-	2	-	-	-	-	-	-
SA-10	1	-	1	-	-	-	-	-	-	-	-
SB-17	37	-	-	30	5	2	-	-	-	-	-
SC-46	1	-	-	-	1	-	-	-	-	-	-
SC-47	1	-	-	-	-	1	-	-	-	-	-
Combat Amphibian	20	6	9	5	-	-	-	-	-	-	-
A-10	19	6	9	4	-	-	-	-	-	-	-
PBY-5	1	-	-	1	-	-	-	-	-	-	-

TABLE 18.— SUMMARY OF USAF AIRCRAFT ON HAND,— INCLUDING AIR RESERVE FORCES AND CIVIL AIR PATROL BY COMMAND AND BY TYPE AND MODEL OF AIRCRAFT: AT END OF EACH QUARTER 1948 -- Continued

Type and Model	Total Overseas (Excl MATS(W/H))	AAC	CairC	FEAF	PAC	USAFE	Misc. Overseas a/	Reserve Forces and CAP			
								Total	AF Reserve	CAP	ANG

31 December 1948 (Contd) — Overseas (Continued)

Type and Model	Total	AAC	CairC	FEAF	PAC	USAFE	Misc.	Total	AF Res	CAP	ANG
Transport - Total	1,029	71	104	294	30	420	110	125	6	-	119
C-74	-	-	-	-	-	-	-	-	-	-	-
C-97	-	-	-	-	-	-	-	-	-	-	-
C-54	28	6	2	15	2	2	1	-	-	-	-
C-112	-	-	-	-	-	-	-	-	-	-	-
C-119	-	-	-	-	-	-	-	-	-	-	-
C-121	-	-	-	-	-	-	-	-	-	-	-
C-46	229	1	-	215	13	-	-	8	6	-	2
C-47	482	45	69	37	1	249	81	114	-	-	114
C-53	8	-	-	-	-	8	-	1	-	-	1
C-82	19	3	-	-	-	-	16	-	-	-	-
CG-17	6	1	2	-	2	-	1	-	-	-	-
VB-17	14	-	2	10	-	2	-	-	-	-	-
CB-25	-	-	-	-	-	-	-	-	-	-	-
VB-25	-	-	-	-	-	-	-	-	-	-	-
CB-26	-	-	-	-	-	-	-	-	-	-	-
VB-26	-	-	-	-	-	-	-	-	-	-	-
C-118	-	-	-	-	-	-	-	-	-	-	-
C-45	192	6	25	15	10	127	9	2	-	-	2
DC-45	7	-	3	2	2	-	-	-	-	-	-
C-64	36	6	-	-	-	30	-	-	-	-	-
C-117	4	-	-	-	-	2	2	-	-	-	-
A-9	1	-	1	-	-	-	-	-	-	-	-
A-12	3	3	-	-	-	-	-	-	-	-	-
Trainer - Total	288	22	48	169	18	25	6	2,019	1,202	387	430
T-6	232	7	15	167	14	24	5	1,133	901	-	232
T-7	10	10	-	-	-	-	-	14	14	-	-
T-11	-	-	-	-	-	-	-	320	285	-	35
TB-17	27	3	22	-	-	1	1	-	-	-	-
TB-25	4	2	-	2	-	-	-	-	-	-	-
TB-26	12	-	8	-	4	-	-	74	2	-	72
TB-29	-	-	-	-	-	-	-	-	-	-	-
TRB-29	-	-	-	-	-	-	-	-	-	-	-
TC-47	-	-	-	-	-	-	-	-	-	-	-
TF-47	-	-	-	-	-	-	-	15	-	-	15
TF-51	-	-	-	-	-	-	-	76	-	-	76
TRF-51	-	-	-	-	-	-	-	-	-	-	-
TF-61	-	-	-	-	-	-	-	-	-	-	-
TF-80	-	-	-	-	-	-	-	-	-	-	-
BT-13	3	-	3	-	-	-	-	-	-	-	-
PT-13	-	-	-	-	-	-	-	387	-	387	-
T-17	-	-	-	-	-	-	-	-	-	-	-
T-19	-	-	-	-	-	-	-	-	-	-	-
Communication - Total	383	24	31	137	11	174	6	255	-	200	55
L-4	28	-	-	28	-	-	-	195	-	195	-
L-5	313	12	21	91	9	174	6	58	-	5	53
L-13	2	2	-	-	-	-	-	-	-	-	-
L-15	-	-	-	-	-	-	-	-	-	-	-
L-16	-	-	-	-	-	-	-	-	-	-	-
L-17	-	-	-	-	-	-	-	2	-	-	2
H-4	-	-	-	-	-	-	-	-	-	-	-
H-5	28	9	10	7	2	-	-	-	-	-	-
H-6	12	1	-	11	-	-	-	-	-	-	-
H-9	-	-	-	-	-	-	-	-	-	-	-
H-10	-	-	-	-	-	-	-	-	-	-	-
H-12	-	-	-	-	-	-	-	-	-	-	-
H-13	-	-	-	-	-	-	-	-	-	-	-
Gliders and Targets	175	11	25	134	5	-	-	-	-	-	-

a/ Includes JBUSMC and AAG

TABLE 19 .-- AIRPLANES ON HAND IN THE USAF, BY MAJOR TYPE: MONTHLY-1948

Note:--Air Reserve and CAP are included in the figures for Jan through Jun and are excluded from the figures for Jul through Dec. Figures are as of end of month.

End of Month	Totals	Heavy Bomber	Medium Bomber	Light Bomber	Fighter	Reconnaissance a/	Transport	Trainer	Communications
1948									
Jan.	23,737	-	2,954	3,388	6,040	655	3,516	5,703	1,481
Feb.	23,686	-	2,958	3,240	6,066	655	3,598	5,691	1,478
Mar.	23,243	-	2,957	3,179	5,968	651	3,521	5,505	1,462
Apr.	22,868	-	2,972	3,131	5,702	651	3,508	5,428	1,476
May.	22,502	-	2,857	3,079	5,565	649	3,463	5,416	1,473
Jun.	22,375	4	2,761	3,078	5,586	642	3,459	5,358	1,487
Jul.	20,099	11	2,043	1,769	4,588	759	3,452	6,276	1,201
Aug.	20,250	15	2,056	1,753	4,582	747	3,669	6,257	1,171
Sep.	20,246	20	2,070	1,772	4,608	745	3,699	6,178	1,154
Oct.	20,328	21	2,073	1,759	4,579	743	3,750	6,247	1,156
Nov.	20,245	25	2,088	1,738	4,539	728	3,748	6,216	1,163
Dec.	20,068	39	2,136	1,700	4,425	731	3,712	6,177	1,148

a/Includes Search and Rescue, Special Research, and Combat Amphibian.

TABLE 20.-- AIRPLANES ON HAND IN THE USAF, BY TYPE AND PRINCIPAL MODEL: MONTHLY-1948

(The data below include Air Reserve and CAP. Figures are as of end of month).

Type and Model	Jan	Feb	Mar	Apr	May	Jun
Total	23,737	23,686	23,243	22,868	22,502	22,375
Combat Airplanes - Total	13,037	12,919	12,755	12,456	12,150	12,071
1st Line	8,874	8,873	8,740	8,468	8,311	8,302
2nd Line & Misc.	4,163	4,046	4,015	3,988	3,839	3,769
Heavy Bomber - Total	-	-	-	-	-	4
1st Line - Total	-	-	-	-	-	3
B-36	-	-	-	-	-	3
2nd Line & Misc.	-	-	-	-	-	1
Medium Bomber - Total	2,954	2,958	2,957	2,972	2,857	2,761
1st Line - Total	2,101	2,099	2,100	2,106	2,106	2,089
B-29	2,095	2,087	2,082	2,087	2,083	2,063
B-50	6	12	18	19	23	26
2nd Line & Misc.	853	859	857	866	751	672
Light Bomber - Total	3,388	3,240	3,179	3,131	3,079	3,078
1st Line - Total	1,181	1,158	1,119	1,115	1,103	1,106
B-45	-	-	-	1	1	3
A-26	1,181	1,158	1,119	1,114	1,102	1,103
2nd Line & Misc.	2,207	2,082	2,060	2,016	1,976	1,972
Fighter - Total	6,040	6,066	5,968	5,702	5,565	5,586
1st Line - Total	5,011	5,040	4,950	4,678	4,535	4,548
P-47	1,976	1,947	1,909	1,661	1,525	1,500
P-51	2,139	2,112	2,038	2,003	1,987	1,953
P-61	190	218	211	203	196	194
P-80	593	595	592	584	583	583
P-82	24	27	26	26	31	57
P-84	89	141	174	201	211	259
P-86	-	-	-	-	2	2
2nd Line & Misc.	1,029	1,026	1,018	1,024	1,030	1,038
Reconnaissance - Total	655	655	651	651	649	640
1st Line - Total	581	576	571	569	567	556
F-9 (FB-17)	74	74	74	74	74	74
FA-26	53	53	52	51	51	51
F-13	88	89	88	88	90	84
F-6	128	123	121	120	119	117
F-15	31	30	30	30	30	30
FP-80	138	137	136	136	135	134
OA-10	69	70	70	70	68	66
2nd Line & Misc.	74	79	80	82	82	84
Special Research - Total	-	-	-	-	-	2
2nd Line & Misc.	-	-	-	-	-	2
Transport - Total	3,516	3,598	3,521	3,508	3,463	3,459
C-97	7	7	7	8	8	8
C-74	12	12	12	12	12	12
C-54	477	477	463	463	462	462
Other Heavy & Med Transport	1	1	1	1	1	3
C-45	659	650	644	636	607	598
C-46	395	495	473	471	472	489
C-47/53	1,698	1,683	1,648	1,635	1,623	1,517
C-82	159	165	169	175	181	186
Other Light Transport	108	108	104	107	97	184
Trainer - Total	5,703	5,691	5,505	5,428	5,416	5,358
Advanced	4,621	4,609	4,480	4,403	4,391	4,357
Basic	66	66	66	66	66	65
Primary	1,016	1,016	959	959	959	936
Communications - Total	1,481	1,478	1,462	1,476	1,473	1,487
Liaison	1,353	1,351	1,339	1,354	1,342	1,348
Rotary Wing	128	127	123	122	131	139

TABLE 20. -- AIRPLANES ON HAND IN THE USAF, BY TYPE AND PRINCIPAL MODEL: MONTHLY-1948
Continued

(The data below exclude Air Reserve and CAP. Figures are as of end of month).

Type and Model	Jul	Aug	Sep	Oct	Nov	Dec
Total	20,099	20,250	20,246	20,328	20,245	20,068
Combat Airplanes - Total	9,170	9,153	9,215	9,175	9,118	9,031
1st Line	4,530	4,588	4,643	4,680	4,714	4,792
2nd Line & Misc.	4,640	4,565	4,572	4,495	4,404	4,239
Heavy Bomber - Total	11	15	20	21	25	39
1st Line - Total	10	14	18	19	23	37
B-36	10	14	18	19	23	37
2nd Line & Misc.	1	1	2	2	2	2
Medium Bomber - Total	2,043	2,056	2,070	2,073	2,088	2,136
1st Line - Total	2,033	2,046	2,036	2,039	2,052	2,092
B-29	2,000	2,007	1,990	1,988	1,992	2,021
B-50	33	39	46	51	60	71
2nd Line & Misc.	10	10	34	34	36	44
Light Bomber - Total	1,769	1,753	1,772	1,759	1,738	1,700
1st Line - Total	1,090	1,088	1,093	1,076	1,061	1,045
B-45	6	8	12	14	14	18
B-26	1,084	1,080	1,081	1,062	1,047	1,027
2nd Line & Misc.	679	665	679	683	677	655
Fighter - Total	4,588	4,582	4,608	4,579	4,539	4,425
1st Line - Total	981	1,044	1,102	1,151	1,188	1,227
F-80	576	610	619	611	604	602
F-82	100	112	135	183	210	231
F-84	301	316	342	349	367	386
F-86	4	6	6	8	7	8
2nd Line & Misc.	3,607	3,538	3,506	3,428	3,351	3,198
Reconnaissance - Total	658	649	644	646	629	630
1st Line - Total	374	372	366	369	362	363
RC-54	-	-	-	1	1	1
RB-26	59	59	59	57	57	57
RB-29	137	136	136	138	137	138
RC-47	-	1	-	-	-	-
RF-80	134	133	131	130	126	126
A-10	44	43	40	43	41	41
2nd Line & Misc.	284	277	278	277	267	267
Special Research - Total	2	2	2	2	2	2
2nd Line & Misc.	2	2	2	2	2	2
Search and Rescue - Total	99	96	99	95	97	99
1st Line - Total	42	24	28	26	28	28
SA-10	18	18	19	16	18	18
Other	24	6	9	10	10	10
2nd Line & Misc.	57	72	71	69	69	71
Transport - Total	3,452	3,669	3,699	3,750	3,748	3,712
C-97	8	8	8	8	8	9
C-74	12	12	12	12	12	12
C-54	459	460	459	458	459	453
Other Hv & Med Transport	3	3	3	3	4	5
C-45	617	615	612	617	612	613
C-46	457	675	694	701	694	679
C-47/53	1,505	1,504	1,498	1,526	1,534	1,517
C-82	196	200	205	206	206	204
Other Light Transport	195	192	208	219	219	220
Trainer - Total	6,276	6,257	6,178	6,247	6,216	6,177
Advanced	5,666	5,646	5,581	5,609	5,578	5,539
Basic	65	65	65	65	65	65
Primary	545	546	532	573	573	573
Communications - Total	1,201	1,171	1,154	1,156	1,163	1,148
Liaison	1,067	1,033	1,017	1,019	1,025	1,008
Helicopter	134	138	137	137	138	140

35

TABLE 21.--AIRPLANES ON HAND IN CONTINENTAL US, BY TYPE AND PRINCIPAL MODEL: MONTHLY-1948

(The data below includes Air Reserve and CAP. Figures are as of end of month).

Type and Model	Jan	Feb	Mar	Apr	May	Jun
Total	18,843	18,831	18,581	18,331	18,100	18,088
Combat Airplanes - Total	10,269	10,263	10,178	10,008	9,772	9,788
1st Line	6,439	6,449	6,391	6,241	6,147	6,229
2nd Line & Misc.	3,830	3,814	3,787	3,767	3,625	3,559
Heavy Bomber - Total	-	-	-	-	-	4
1st Line Total	-	-	-	-	-	3
B-36	-	-	-	-	-	3
2nd Line and Misc.	-	-	-	-	-	1
Medium Bomber - Total	2,873	2,874	2,844	2,840	2,729	2,635
1st Line Total	2,020	2,016	1,988	1,975	1,978	1,964
B-29	2,014	2,004	1,970	1,956	1,955	1,938
B-50	6	12	18	19	23	26
2nd Line & Misc.	853	858	856	865	751	671
Light Bomber - Total	2,873	2,827	2,798	2,757	2,715	2,720
1st Line - Total	981	958	947	943	934	938
B-45	-	-	-	1	1	3
A-26	981	958	947	942	933	935
2nd Line & Misc.	1,892	1,869	1,851	1,814	1,781	1,782
Fighter - Total	4,094	4,136	4,118	3,993	3,915	4,022
1st Line - Total	3,066	3,111	3,101	2,970	2,886	2,985
P-47	989	990	954	915	900	894
P-51	1,459	1,446	1,442	1,369	1,324	1,331
P-61	107	107	107	100	94	92
P-80	398	401	398	359	324	350
P-82	24	27	26	26	31	57
P-84	89	140	174	201	211	259
P-86	-	-	-	-	2	2
2nd Line & Misc.	1,028	1,025	1,017	1,023	1,029	1,037
Reconnaissance - Total	429	426	418	418	413	405
1st Line - Total	372	364	355	353	349	339
F-9 (FB-17)	27	27	26	26	26	26
FA-26	44	44	43	43	43	43
F-13	71	72	69	69	68	64
F-6	74	72	71	70	69	67
F-15	7	6	6	6	3	3
FP-80	107	101	100	100	100	99
OA-10	42	42	40	39	40	37
2nd Line & Misc.	57	62	63	65	64	66
Special Research - Total	-	-	-	-	-	2
2nd Line & Misc.	-	-	-	-	-	2
Transport - Total	2,163	2,168	2,169	2,142	2,159	2,192
C-97	7	7	7	8	8	8
C-74	12	12	12	12	12	11
C-54	313	317	311	306	301	291
Other Hv. & Med Transport	1	1	1	1	1	3
C-45	419	419	414	407	407	406
C-46	152	152	152	153	176	202
C-47/53	1,089	1,081	1,073	1,066	1,058	1,057
C-82	143	149	169	157	164	182
Other Light Transport	27	30	30	32	32	32
Trainer - Total	5,419	5,394	5,228	5,154	5,143	5,088
Advanced	4,355	4,330	4,221	4,147	4,136	4,104
Basic	62	62	62	62	62	62
Primary	1,002	1,002	945	945	945	922
Communications - Total	992	1,006	1,006	1,027	1,026	1,020
Liaison	899	914	922	944	934	925
Rotary Wing	93	92	84	83	92	95

TABLE 21.-- AIRPLANES ON HAND IN CONTINENTAL US, BY TYPE AND PRINCIPAL MODEL: MONTHLY-1948-Continued

(The data below exclude Air Reserve and CAP. Figures are as of end of month).

Type and Model	Jul	Aug	Sep	Oct	Nov	Dec
Total	15,833	16,057	16,077	16,133	16,015	15,975
Combat Airplanes - Total	6,937	6,977	7,069	7,022	6,954	6,981
1st Line	3,790	3,859	3,890	3,888	3,885	4,028
2nd Line & Misc.	3,147	3,118	3,179	3,134	3,069	2,953
Heavy Bomber Total	11	15	20	21	25	39
1st Line - Total	10	14	18	19	23	37
B-36	10	14	18	19	23	37
2nd Line & Misc.	1	1	2	2	2	2
Medium Bomber - Total	1,862	1,882	1,894	1,891	1,872	1,980
1st Line - Total	1,852	1,872	1,860	1,857	1,834	1,937
B-29	1,819	1,833	1,814	1,806	1,780	1,869
B-50	33	39	46	51	54	68
2nd Line & Misc.	10	10	34	34	38	43
Light Bomber - Total	1,535	1,541	1,561	1,559	1,537	1,498
1st Line - Total	933	938	943	929	915	897
B-45	6	8	12	14	14	18
B-26	927	930	931	915	901	879
2nd Line & Misc.	602	603	618	630	622	601
Fighter - Total	3,114	3,129	3,186	3,150	3,120	3,056
1st Line - Total	733	776	810	831	866	905
F-80	328	342	327	303	300	298
F-82	100	112	135	171	193	214
F-84	301	316	342	349	366	385
F-86	4	6	6	8	7	8
2nd Line & Misc.	2,381	2,353	2,376	2,319	2,254	2,151
Reconnaissance - Total	381	376	375	369	363	368
1st Line - Total	249	246	245	238	233	238
RB-29	87	86	86	81	78	83
RB-26	43	43	43	41	41	41
RF-80	99	98	98	97	93	93
RC-54	-	-	-	1	1	1
RC-47	-	1	-	-	-	-
A-10	20	18	18	18	20	20
2nd Line & Misc.	132	130	130	131	130	130
Special Research - Total	2	2	2	2	2	2
2nd Line - Total	2	2	2	2	2	2
X-1	2	2	2	2	2	2
Search and Rescue - Total	32	32	31	30	35	38
1st Line - Total	13	13	14	14	14	14
SA-10	13	13	14	14	14	14
Other	-	-	-	-	-	-
2nd Line & Misc.	19	19	17	16	21	24
Transport - Total	2,142	2,372	2,367	2,411	2,384	2,360
C-97	8	8	8	8	8	9
C-74	12	12	12	12	12	12
C-54	252	234	213	239	220	194
Other Hv & Med Transport	3	3	3	3	4	5
C-45 (DC-45)	423	419	417	416	412	413
C-46	178	426	453	459	452	444
C-47/53	965	964	955	951	949	954
C-82	177	182	167	162	182	180
Other Light Transport	124	124	139	141	145	149
Trainer - Total	5,961	5,939	5,876	5,945	5,916	5,878
Advanced	5,368	5,345	5,282	5,310	5,281	5,243
Basic	62	62	62	62	62	62
Primary	531	532	532	573	573	573
Communications - Total	793	769	765	755	761	756
Liaison	692	668	662	656	662	658
Helicopter	101	101	103	99	99	98

847201 O - 49 - 4

TABLE 22 .-- AIRPLANES ON HAND OVERSEAS, BY TYPE AND PRINCIPAL MODEL: MONTHLY 1948

Note:—The data below do not reflect changes for a particular month resulting from information becoming available subsequent to the reporting cut-off date for that month. Figures are as of end of month.

Type and Model	Jan	Feb	Mar	Apr	May	Jun
Total	4,894	4,855	4,662	4,537	4,402	4,287
Combat Airplanes - Total	2,768	2,656	2,577	2,448	2,378	2,283
1st Line	2,435	2,424	2,349	2,227	2,164	2,073
2nd Line & Misc	333	232	228	221	214	210
Medium Bomber - Total	81	84	113	132	129	126
1st Line - Total	81	83	112	131	128	125
B-29	81	83	112	131	128	125
2nd Line & Misc	-	1	1	1	1	1
Light Bomber - Total	515	413	381	374	363	358
1st Line - Total	200	200	172	172	169	168
A-26	200	200	172	172	169	168
2nd Line & Misc	315	213	209	202	194	190
Fighter - Total	1,946	1,930	1,850	1,709	1,650	1,564
1st Line - Total	1,945	1,929	1,849	1,708	1,649	1,563
P-47	987	957	955	746	625	606
P-51	680	666	596	634	663	622
P-61	83	111	104	103	102	102
P-80	195	194	194	225	259	233
P-84	-	1	-	-	-	-
2nd Line & Misc	1	1	1	1	1	1
Reconnaissance - Total	226	229	233	233	236	235
1st Line - Total	209	212	216	216	218	217
F-9 (FB-17)	47	47	48	48	48	48
FA-26	9	9	9	8	8	8
F-13	17	17	19	19	22	20
F-6	54	51	50	50	50	50
F-15	24	24	24	24	27	27
FP-80	31	36	36	36	35	35
OA-10	27	28	30	31	28	29
2nd Line & Misc	17	17	17	17	18	18
Transport - Total	1,352	1,430	1,352	1,366	1,304	1,267
C-74	-	-	-	-	-	1
C-54	164	160	152	157	161	171
C-45	240	231	230	229	200	192
C-46	243	343	321	318	296	288
C-47/53	609	602	575	569	565	550
C-82	16	16	-	18	17	4
Other Light Transport	81	78	74	75	65	61
Trainer - Total	284	297	277	274	273	270
Advanced	266	279	259	256	255	253
Basic	4	4	4	4	4	3
Primary	14	14	14	14	14	14
Communications - Total	489	472	456	449	447	467
Liaison	454	437	417	410	408	423
Rotary Wing	35	35	39	39	39	44

TABLE 22 .-- AIRPLANES ON HAND OVERSEAS, BY TYPE AND PRINCIPAL MODEL: MONTHLY, 1948--Continued

Note:--The data below do not reflect changes for a particular month resulting from information becoming available subsequent to the reporting cut-off date for that month. Figures are as of end of month.

Type and Model	Jul	Aug	Sep	Oct	Nov	Dec
Total	4,266	4,193	4,169	4,195	4,230	4,093
Combat Airplanes - Total	2,233	2,176	2,146	2,153	2,164	2,050
1st Line	740	729	753	792	829	764
2nd Line & Misc.	1,493	1,447	1,393	1,361	1,335	1,286
Medium Bomber - Total	181	174	176	182	218	156
1st Line - Total	181	174	176	182	218	155
B-29	181	174	176	182	212	152
B-50	-	-	-	-	6	3
2nd Line & Misc.	-	-	-	-	-	1
Light Bomber - Total	234	212	211	200	199	202
1st Line - Total	157	150	150	147	146	148
B-26	157	150	150	147	146	148
2nd Line & Misc.	77	62	61	53	53	54
Fighter - Total	1,474	1,453	1,422	1,429	1,419	1,369
1st Line - Total	248	268	292	320	322	322
F-80	248	268	292	308	304	304
F-82	-	-	-	12	17	17
F-84	-	-	-	-	1	1
2nd Line & Misc.	1,226	1,185	1,130	1,109	1,097	1,047
Reconnaissance - Total	277	273	269	277	266	262
1st Line Total	125	126	121	131	129	125
RB-29	50	50	50	57	59	55
RB-26	16	16	16	16	16	16
RF-80	35	35	33	33	33	33
A-10	24	25	22	25	21	21
2nd Line & Misc.	152	147	148	146	137	137
Search and Rescue - Total	67	64	68	65	62	61
1st Line - Total	29	13	14	12	14	14
SA-10	5	5	5	2	4	4
Other	24	8	9	10	10	10
2nd Line & Misc.	38	51	54	53	48	47
Transport - Total	1,310	1,297	1,332	1,339	1,364	1,352
C-54	207	226	246	219	239	259
Other Hv & Med Transp.	-	-	-	-	-	-
C-45	194	196	195	201	200	200
C-46	279	249	241	242	242	235
C-47/53	550	540	543	575	585	563
C-82	19	18	18	24	24	24
Other Light Transp	61	68	69	78	74	71
Trainer - Total	315	318	302	302	300	299
Advanced	298	301	299	299	297	296
Basic	3	3	3	3	3	3
Primary	14	14	-	-	-	-
Communications - Total	408	402	389	401	402	392
Liaison	375	365	355	363	363	350
Helicopter	33	37	34	38	39	42

TABLE 23.-- AIRPLANES ON HAND IN THE USAF ACCOUNTABLE INVENTORY, BY TYPE

| Line No. | Type and Model | Airplanes On Hand 31 Dec 47 | Gains |||||
			Production	Operational a/	Class 01Z	Air National Guard	United States Army
1	Total	23,814	412	239	21	17	136
2	Bomber - Total	6,404	32	40	3	10	-
3	B-36	-	4	-	-	-	-
4	B-29	2,969	-	27	2	-	-
5	B-50	3	23	-	-	-	-
6	B-17	570	-	10	-	-	-
7	B-25	1,375	-	2	1	-	-
8	B-45	-	3	-	-	-	-
9	A-26	1,463	-	1	-	10	-
10	Other	24	2	-	-	-	-
11	Fighter - Total	6,053	289	60	13	2	-
12	P-47	2,431	-	14	-	2	-
13	P-51	2,359	-	17	10	1	-
14	P-61	214	-	28	-	-	-
15	P-80	635	35	1	3	-	-
16	P-82	25	39	-	-	-	-
17	P-84	75	212	-	-	-	-
18	P-86	-	2	-	-	-	-
19	Other	314	1	-	-	-	-
20	Reconnaissance - Total	661	1	3	-	-	-
21	F-9 (FB-17)	74	-	-	-	-	-
22	FA-26	52	-	-	-	-	-
23	F-13	96	-	2	-	-	-
24	F-6	146	-	-	-	-	-
25	F-15	31	-	-	-	-	-
26	FP-80	140	-	-	-	-	-
27	OA-10	68	-	1	-	-	-
28	Other	54	1	-	-	-	-
29	Special Research - Total	-	2	-	-	-	-
30	XS-1	-	2	-	-	-	-
31	Transport - Total	3,536	38	125	1	1	-
32	C-97	7	1	-	-	-	-
33	C-74	12	-	-	-	-	-
34	C-54	477	-	1	-	-	-
35	Other Hv & Med Transport . . .	1	2	-	-	-	-
36	C-45	663	-	3	-	-	-
37	C-46	396	-	118	1	1	-
38	C-47/53	1,715	-	2	-	-	-
39	C-82	153	35	1	-	-	-
40	Other Light Transport	112	-	-	-	-	-
41	Trainer - Total	5,714	-	3	-	3	-
42	Advanced	4,631	-	3	-	3	-
43	Basic & Primary	1,083	-	-	-	-	-
44	Communications - Total	1,446	50	8	4	-	136
45	Liaison	1,318	38	6	4	-	128
46	Rotary Wing	128	12	2	-	-	8

a/ Includes salvage.
b/ Includes gains or losses from or to other non-USAF agencies and various other inventory adjustments.

AND PRINCIPAL MODEL, SHOWING GAINS AND LOSSES: 31 DEC 1947 TO 30 JUNE 1948

Gains (Contd)	Losses						Airplanes On Hand 30 Jun 1948	Line No.
Miscel- laneous b/	Oper- ational a/	Air National Guard	WAA FLC	United States Army	Class 01Z	Miscel- laneous b/		
4,602	1,282	159	292	53	66	5,014	22,375	1
1031	520	53	33	–	2	1,062	5,843	2
–	–	–	–	–	–	–	4	3
51	260	–	–	–	4	50	2,735	4
–	–	–	–	–	–	–	26	5
402	206	–	–	–	–	404	372	6
548	21	–	33	–	5	548	1,319	7
–	–	–	–	–	–	–	3	8
19	29	53	–	–	–	48	1,363	9
11	4	–	–	–	–	12	21	10
284	354	94	112	10	19	527	5,586	11
171	193	75	3	10	2	411	1,924	12
27	87	19	109	–	8	28	2,163	13
65	36	–	–	–	1	65	205	14
14	25	–	–	–	6	14	643	15
–	3	–	–	–	–	1	60	16
2	10	–	–	–	2	2	275	17
–	–	–	–	–	–	–	2	18
5	–	–	–	–	–	6	314	19
132	26	–	1	–	–	130	640	20
46	–	–	–	–	–	46	74	21
1	1	–	–	–	–	1	51	22
2	10	–	–	–	–	3	87	23
25	5	–	–	–	–	25	141	24
1	–	–	–	–	–	1	31	25
1	5	–	–	–	–	1	135	26
10	4	–	1	–	–	8	66	27
46	1	–	–	–	–	45	55	28
–	–	–	–	–	–	–	2	29
–	–	–	–	–	–	–	2	30
226	177	7	117	1	4	162	3,459	31
–	–	–	–	–	–	–	8	32
–	–	–	–	–	–	–	12	33
–	16	–	–	–	–	–	462	34
–	–	–	–	–	–	–	3	35
8	24	–	41	–	–	11	598	36
74	78	–	19	–	1	2	490	37
37	51	7	35	–	2	52	1,607	38
–	2	–	–	–	1	–	186	39
107	6	–	22	1	–	97	93	40
2,344	121	5	2	31	–	2,547	5,358	41
1,262	70	5	2	–	–	1,465	4,357	42
1,082	51	–	–	31	–	1,082	1,001	43
585	84	–	27	11	34	586	1,487	44
582	74	–	27	11	34	582	1,348	45
3	10	–	–	–	–	4	139	46

TABLE 24. -- AIRPLANES ON HAND IN THE USAF ACCOUNTABLE INVENTORY, BY TYPE AND

| Line No. | Type and Model | Airplanes On Hand 30 Jun 48 | Gains |||||
			Pro-duction	Oper-ational a/	Class OIZ	Air National Guard	United States Army
1	Total	22,375	599	19	11	7	29
2	Bomber - Total	5,843	107	2	2	2	-
3	B-36	4	35	-	-	-	-
4	B-29	2,735	-	1	2	-	-
5	B-50	26	47	-	-	-	-
6	B-35	-	2	-	-	-	-
7	B-17	372	-	1	-	-	-
8	B-25	1,319	-	-	-	-	-
9	B-45	3	20	-	-	2	-
10	B-26	1,363	-	-	-	-	-
11	Other	21	3	-	-	-	-
12	Fighter - Total	5,586	425	6	1	1	-
13	F-47	1,924	-	1	-	1	-
14	F-51	2,163	-	-	-	-	-
15	F-61	205	-	1	-	-	-
16	F-80	643	78	1	1	-	-
17	F-82	60	189	1	-	-	-
18	F-84	275	146	2	-	-	-
19	F-86	2	11	-	-	-	-
20	Other	314	1	-	-	-	-
21	Reconnaissance - Total	574	2	-	-	1	-
22	J-17	74	-	-	-	-	-
23	RB-26	51	-	-	-	-	-
24	RB-29	87	-	-	-	-	-
25	RF-51	141	-	-	-	-	-
26	RF-61	31	-	-	-	-	-
27	RF-80	135	-	-	-	1	-
28	Other	55	2	-	-	-	-
29	Search & Rescue - Total	-	-	-	-	-	-
30	SA-10	-	-	-	-	-	-
31	Other	-	-	-	-	-	-
32	Combat Amphibian - Total	66	-	-	-	-	-
33	A-10	66	-	-	-	-	-
34	Other	-	-	-	-	-	-
35	Special Research - Total	2	-	-	-	-	-
36	X-1	2	-	-	-	-	-
37	Transport - Total	3,459	25	7	3	-	6
38	C-97	8	1	-	-	-	-
39	C-74	12	-	-	-	-	-
40	C-54	462	-	4	2	-	-
41	Other Heavy & Medium Transport	3	2	-	-	-	-
42	C-45	598	-	-	-	-	-
43	C-46	490	-	2	-	-	-
44	C-47/53	1,607	-	1	1	-	6
45	C-82	186	22	-	-	-	-
46	Other Light Transport	93	-	-	-	-	-
47	Trainer - Total	5,358	20	3	1	3	-
48	Advanced	4,357	20	3	1	3	-
49	Basic & Primary	1,001	-	-	-	-	-
50	Communications - Total	1,487	20	1	4	-	23
51	Liaison	1,348	2	1	4	-	19
52	Helicopter	139	18	-	-	-	4

a/ Includes salvage.
b/ Includes gains or losses from or to other non-USAF agencies and various other inventory adjustments.

PRINCIPAL MODEL, SHOWING GAINS AND LOSSES: 30 JUNE 1948 TO 31 DEC 1948

Gains (Contd) Miscellaneous b/	Operational a/	Air National Guard	Losses WAA FLC	United States Army	Class 012	Miscellaneous b/	Airplanes On Hand 31 Dec 48	Line No.
9,326	802	98	244	38	24	9,255	21,905	1
189	81	1	-	-	4	2,142	3,917	2
1	-	-	-	-	-	1	39	3
114	50	-	-	-	2	742	2,058	4
2	-	-	-	-	-	2	73	5
-	-	-	-	-	-	-	2	6
30	16	-	-	-	1	231	155	7
14	2	-	-	-	-	856	475	8
-	1	-	-	-	1	-	21	9
28	7	1	-	-	-	301	1,084	10
-	5	-	-	-	-	9	10	11
284	283	95	194	-	8	1,293	4,425	12
5	84	16	95	-	-	427	1,309	13
23	45	79	99	-	2	248	1,713	14
199	84	-	-	-	-	205	116	15
25	35	-	-	-	2	78	633	16
9	8	-	-	-	-	9	242	17
16	28	-	-	-	1	16	394	18
-	-	-	-	-	2	1	10	19
7	4	-	-	-	1	309	8	20
368	19	1	8	-	1	328	588	21
8	3	-	-	-	-	5	74	22
61	-	-	-	-	-	53	59	23
143	-	-	-	-	-	91	139	24
121	5	-	8	-	1	144	104	25
31	2	-	-	-	-	31	29	26
-	8	1	-	-	-	-	127	27
4	1	-	-	-	-	4	56	28
142	5	-	-	-	-	38	99	29
22	1	-	-	-	-	3	18	30
120	4	-	-	-	-	35	81	31
69	5	-	-	-	-	88	42	32
69	5	-	-	-	-	88	42	33
-	-	-	-	-	-	-	-	34
-	-	-	-	-	-	-	2	35
-	-	-	-	-	-	-	2	36
687	173	-	26	-	-	270	1,718	37
-	-	-	-	-	-	-	9	38
-	-	-	-	-	-	-	12	39
14	13	-	-	-	-	16	453	40
-	-	-	-	-	-	-	5	41
41	16	-	-	-	-	10	613	42
286	83	-	-	-	-	3	685	43
129	40	-	7	-	-	169	1,517	44
4	4	-	18	-	-	4	204	45
213	17	-	1	-	-	68	220	46
7,243	118	-	15	1	2	4,726	7,766	47
7,059	118	-	1	1	2	4,580	6,741	48
184	-	-	14	-	-	146	1,025	49
344	113	1	1	37	9	370	1,348	50
194	95	1	1	37	8	218	1,208	51
150	18	-	-	-	1	152	140	52

TABLE 25 -- CUMULATIVE AGE DISTRIBUTION OF THE USAF AIRPLANE INVENTORY: AS OF 30 NOVEMBER 1948

Age in Months Less than	Bomber Heavy	Bomber Medium	Bomber Light	Fighter Jet	Fighter Pen. & Intcp.	Fighter All Weather	Transport Heavy	Transport Medium	Transport Light	Trainer	All Others
6	24	41	15	237	67	107	–	2	23	14	20
12	25	63	16	437	91	108	1	3	63	14	104
18		65	19	658	95	108	5	4	102	14	170
24		65	20	685	95	108	15	4	144	14	253
30		65	21	819	95	108	18	4	181	27	354
36		86	22	925	112	113	19	6	215	57	380
42		939	378	1,010	1,467	141	20	256	725	856	740
48		1,896	1,503	1,015	3,056	202		460	1,514	2,408	1,315
54		2,090	1,710		3,262	248		460	2,613	3,790	1,484
60			1,733		3,269	251		462	3,054	4,590	1,618
66			1,735		3,271			462	3,215	5,262	1,773
72			1,736		3,272			463	3,258	5,712	1,855
78					3,273				3,263	6,011	1,874
84									3,264	6,116	1,890
90										6,192	1,890
96										6,214	1,890
102										6,215	1,890
108										6,215	1,891
114										6,216	
120									3,265		

TABLE 26.-- AIRPLANES ON HAND IN USAF DURING 1948: ACTIVE AND INACTIVE

Note:-- Inactive airplanes include storage and excess airplanes for period, Jan-Jun and also aircraft on bailment contract, those on loan to non-USAF agencies, and "X" prefixed models for period, Jul-Dec. In addition, data for Jan-Jun include Air Reserve and Civil Air Patrol.

End of Month	Total USAF				Continental US				Overseas			
	Total	Active	Inactive Storage	Inactive Other	Total	Active	Inactive Storage	Inactive Other	Total	Active	Inactive Storage	Inactive Other
1948												
Jan	23,737	11,393	10,945	1,399	18,843	8,442	9,894	507	4,894	2,951	1,051	892
Feb	23,686	11,577	10,686	1,423	18,831	8,496	9,811	524	4,855	3,081	875	899
Mar	23,243	11,660	10,564	1,019	18,581	8,593	9,710	278	4,662	3,067	854	741
Apr	22,868	11,766	10,277	825	18,331	8,662	9,510	159	4,537	3,104	767	666
May	22,502	11,831	9,966	705	18,100	8,654	9,315	131	4,402	3,177	651	574
Jun	22,375	11,856	9,855	664	18,088	8,723	9,224	141	4,287	3,133	631	523
Jul	20,099	9,838	9,265	996	15,833	6,629	8,676	528	4,266	3,209	589	468
Aug	20,250	9,787	9,328	1,135	16,057	6,722	8,777	558	4,193	3,065	551	577
Sep	20,246	9,763	9,283	1,200	16,077	6,742	8,737	598	4,169	3,021	546	602
Oct	20,328	9,784	9,277	1,267	16,133	6,749	8,736	648	4,195	3,035	541	619
Nov	20,245	9,813	9,271	1,161	16,015	6,691	8,769	555	4,230	3,122	502	606
Dec	20,068	9,692	9,090	1,286	15,975	6,701	8,734	540	4,093	2,991	356	746

TABLE 27 -- VALUE OF AIRCRAFT PARTS IN INVENTORY AND ON-ORDER, BY PROPERTY CLASSIFICATION AND AIRPLANE MANUFACTURER OR MAJOR COMPONENT INVOLVED: AS OF JAN 1948 AND JAN 1949

Note: Inventory figures include both active and inactive materials held for possible diversion to Foreign Aid Programs. Values of on-order materials include both initial spares and replenishment for aircraft already in service.

Property Class	Manufacturer or Major Component	Jan 1948 Value Inv.	Jan 1949 Value Inv.	Jan. 1948 Value On Order	Jan 1949 Value On Order
	Total	$1,392,941,336	$1,264,955,388	$132,032,923	$227,137,473
	Airframe Parts - Total	221,726,340	219,283,975	52,812,341	56,731,766
01-B	Consolidated	8,309,711	8,793,565	1,171,057	3,377,655
01-C	Curtiss	21,493,982	20,000,000	124,008	9,326
01-D	Douglas	45,620,555	43,209,438	12,304,606	10,018,733
01-E	Northrop.	1,523,609	1,611,804	271,688	1,800,000
01-F	Boeing	59,467,713	60,500,000	17,872,651	15,002,937
01-G	Misc.	2,219,419	1,198,300	962,486	753,195
01-H	Beech	8,415,044	5,729,170	3,397,597	319,621
01-J	Naco	4,817,674	2,814,150	0	0
01-L	Lockheed	5,021,261	5,490,946	2,733,068	919,319
01-M	North American	37,607,018	43,607,018	9,993,232	11,993,232
01-N	Republic	22,284,161	22,545,318	3,048,444	11,050,000
01-R	Fairchild	1,238,133	2,816,966	637,372	1,287,408
01-J	Bell	92,508	702,563	149,783	180,490
01-O	Piper, Aeronca, Taylor	615,552	264,737	146,349	19,850
	Components & Related Spare Parts-Total	1,171,214,996	1,045,671,413	79,220,582	170,405,707
02-B	Auxiliary Aircraft Engines . . .	7,510,507	6,953,000	0	255,000
02-C	Spare parts for Continental Engines	8,817,017	8,973,000	39,387	120,000
02-D	Spare parts for Wright Engines. . .	134,667,463	132,543,000	2,789,080	9,752,000
02-E	Spare parts for Lycoming Engines.	8,856,026	8,833,000	119,313	500
02-H	Spare parts for Pratt & Whitney . .	119,452,479	115,450,000	8,656,605	12,344,000
02-I	Spare parts for Allison Engines . .	11,828,961	11,661,000	238,073	101,000
02-J	Spare parts for Packard Engines . .	20,590,492	18,736,900	281,605	519,000
02-F	Spare parts for Franklin Engines. .	742,575	710,000	157,098	25,000
02-Q	Spare parts for Jet Engines . . .	10,830,769	15,830,000	16,198,549	43,120,000
03-A	Propellers and Related Parts . . .	105,084,230	97,100,000	4,860,194	10,115,000
03-B	Wheels and Brakes Parts	21,925,313	23,700,000	7,440,349	8,250,000
03-C	Aircraft Electrical Equipment . . .	131,732,831	101,225,000	5,410,477	9,185,000
03-D	Carburators	34,003,297	36,400,000	2,788,534	11,750,000
03-E	Superchargers	19,711,888	21,435,000	1,564,377	2,157,000
03-F	Misc. Aircraft Accessories	19,218,440	26,650,000	3,054,229	7,500,000
03-G	Hydraulic Struts	20,299,322	16,375,000	2,015,476	6,560,000
03-H	Ignition Systems	68,604,432	61,600,000	6,132,217	4,927,000
03-I	Hydraulic, Fuel, Vacuum Systems . .	70,206,582	53,400,000	4,557,353	7,100,000
03-J	Aircraft Engine Accessories . . .	10,041,522	9,800,000	1,393,247	2,800,000
03-K	Breathing Oxygen Equipment	14,939,895	13,200,000	156,158	150,000
03-L	Auxiliary Tanks	a/	1,200,000	a/	6,950,000
03-M	Transmission Systems	1,069,299	2,120,000	3,254,623	1,800,000
04-A	Aircraft Hardware	28,735,175	24,640,000	2,536,188	4,811,700
04-B	Rubber Mat. (Tubs & Casings Exc). .	3,654,295	1,975,420	1,167,226	5,128,828
04-C	Tubes and Casings	18,944,549	17,731,712	1,832,637	2,305,963
05-A	Navigation Instruments	19,117,664	10,675,000	14,488	325,000
05-C	Flight Instruments	54,129,216	42,225,000	157,385	3,045,000
05-D	Engine Instruments	14,823,820	13,300,000	212,098	1,800,000
05-E	Instruments Maintenance Parts . . .	8,551,984	6,750,000	240,539	1,350,000
05-F	Auto-Pilots and Gyros	21,572,956	17,350,000	820,938	3,500,000
05-G	Miscellaneous Instruments	7,702,263	5,550,000	397,295	1,450,000
11-A	Bombing Equipment	83,295,526	64,177,070	106,919	875,564
11-B	Gunnery Equipment	11,839,323	7,527,924	368,960	51,625
11-D	Local Fire Control	2,152,901	2,100,000	0	0
11-E	Central Fire Control	49,862,114	40,500,000	128,417	271,527
11-F	Guided Missiles	6,669,850	6,915,227	0	0

a/ Class 03-L January 1948 values not available as items were procured for specific requirements and no stocks were maintained for support.

Source: Office of Director of Maintenance, Supply and Services - Supply Division - DCS/M.

TABLE 28.--AIRPLANE LOSSES IN CONTINENTAL US AND OVERSEAS, BY TYPE OF AIRPLANE: MONTHLY, 1948

(Figures in parentheses indicate the excess of gains from salvage over losses)

Type of Airplane	Total	Jan	Feb	Mar	Apr	May	Jun	Jul	Aug	Sep	Oct	Nov	Dec
Total USAF	1,868	140	42	198	180	295	224	245	170	100	71	90	113
Very Heavy Bomber	-	-	-	-	-	-	-	-	-	-	-	-	-
Heavy Bomber	-	-	-	-	-	-	-	-	-	-	-	-	-
Medium Bomber	286	22	2	7	(14)	119	100	33	4	3	6	2	2
Light Bomber	282	21	109	19	49	45	7	6	6	4	5	9	2
Fighter	550	55	1	16	81	83	25	72	67	35	31	30	54
Other	750	42	(70)	156	64	48	92	134	93	58	29	49	55
Total Continental US	1,106	42	38	102	128	198	174	133	84	47	51	59	50
Very Heavy Bomber	-	-	-	-	-	-	-	-	-	-	-	-	-
Heavy Bomber	-	-	-	-	-	-	-	-	-	-	-	-	-
Medium Bomber	257	4	5	7	2	116	90	27	3	(1)	-	2	2
Light Bomber	117	6	7	7	44	40	4	-	1	2	3	2	1
Fighter	208	10	13	(16)	32	13	11	34	24	17	23	23	24
Other	524	22	13	104	50	29	69	72	56	29	25	32	23
Total Overseas	762	98	4	96	52	97	50	112	86	53	20	31	63
Very Heavy Bomber	-	-	-	-	-	-	-	-	-	-	-	-	-
Heavy Bomber	-	-	-	-	-	-	-	-	-	-	-	-	-
Medium Bomber	29	18	(3)	-	(16)	3	10	6	1	4	6	-	-
Light Bomber	165	15	102	12	5	5	3	6	5	2	2	7	1
Fighter	342	45	(12)	32	49	70	14	38	43	18	8	7	30
Other	226	20	(83)	52	14	19	23	62	37	29	4	17	32

TABLE 29. -- AIRCRAFT IN STORAGE AT AIR MATERIEL COMMAND INSTALLATIONS, IN CONTINENTAL US, BY TYPE OF AIRPLANE: MONTHLY-1948

End of Month	Total	Medium Bomber a/	Light Bomber a/	Fighter	Cargo	Trainer	Misc. Types b/	Glider, Target
Jan	10,246	2,417	1,462	2,533	365	2,507	457	505
Feb	10,165	2,413	1,527	2,567	356	2,353	450	499
Mar	10,045	2,389	1,547	2,592	370	2,224	432	491
Apr	9,869	2,285	1,526	2,537	386	2,211	433	491
May	9,641	2,053	1,479	2,559	381	2,257	421	491
Jun	9,529	1,908	1,479	2,556	400	2,272	423	491
Jul	9,437	1,818	1,585	2,543	360	2,262	425	444
Aug	9,384	1,801	1,424	2,547	591	2,177	399	445
Sep	9,285	1,796	1,412	2,546	575	2,118	393	445
Oct	9,194	1,788	1,389	2,531	557	2,096	388	445
Nov	9,076	1,782	1,337	2,509	550	2,060	393	445
Dec	9,062	1,772	1,317	2,529	520	2,145	409	370

a/ Medium Bombers - B-29; Light Bombers - A-26 (as of 1 Jul 48, A-26 became B-26), B-25, and B-17.

b/ Includes Liaison, Rotary Wing and Amphibious Planes.

Source: Cost Control and Analysis Office, Comptroller's Department, Hq., Air Materiel Command.

TABLE 30.—USAF OWNED OR LEASED BULK PETROLEUM STORAGE CAPACITY, BY AREA AND PRODUCT: 3RD AND 4TH QUARTER-1948

(In thousands of barrels. Excluding tanks with less than 500 barrel capacity)

THIRD QUARTER

Area and Product	Total	In Use	Not in Use	Re-pairable (Not in use)	Abandoned (not Re-pairable)	Area and Product	Total	In Use	Not in Use	Re-pairable (Not in use)	Abandoned (Not Re-pairable)
WORLD-Total	2107	1662	355	52	38	CARIB (contd)					
Avgas	1490	1133	303	40	14	Mogas	29	25	4	-	-
Jet Fuel	73	73	-	-	-	Diesel	33	31	1	1	-
Mogas	125	110	5	10	0	Other	5	4	-	1	-
Diesel	352	325	3	1	23						
Fuel Oil	17	17	-	-	-	EUCOM	7	7	-	-	-
Other	5	4	-	1	-	Avgas	7	7	-	-	-
Empty	45	-	44	-	1						
						CINCAL	731	654	41	10	26
OFF-SHORE-Total	2049	1608	351	52	38	Avgas	431	389	39	-	3
Avgas	1438	1081	303	40	14	Mogas	55	45	-	10	-
Jet Fuel	73	73	-	-	-	Diesel	245	220	2	0	23
Mogas	125	110	5	10	-						
Diesel	352	325	3	1	23	CINCPAC	173	116	33	22	2
Fuel Oil	15	15	-	-	-	Avgas	168	113	32	22	1
Other	5	4	-	1	-	Mogas	2	1	1	-	-
Empty	41	0	40	-	1	Diesel	2	2	-	-	-
						Empty	1	-	-	-	1
CINCFE	398	255	142	-	1						
Avgas	280	177	102	-	1	ON-SHORE-Total	58	54	4	-	-
Jet Fuel	61	61	-	-	-	Avgas	52	52	-	-	-
Mogas	13	13	-	-	-	Fuel Oil	2	2	-	-	-
Diesel	4	4	-	-	-	Empty	4	-	4	-	-
Empty	40	-	40	-	-						
						EAST COAST	32	28	4	-	-
NORLANT	232	231	-	-	1	Avgas	26	26	-	-	-
Avgas	111	110	-	-	1	Fuel Oil	2	2	-	-	-
Jet Fuel	12	12	-	-	-	Empty	4	-	4	-	-
Mogas	26	26	-	-	-						
Diesel	68	68	-	-	-	INLAND	2	2	-	-	-
Fuel Oil	15	15	-	-	-	Avgas	2	2	-	-	-
Empty	-	-	-	-	-						
						GULF COAST	24	24	-	-	-
CARIB	508	343	115	20	8	Avgas	24	24	-	-	-
Avgas	441	285	130	18	8						

FOURTH QUARTER

Area and Product	Total	In Use	Not in Use	Repairable (not in use)	Abandoned (Not re-pairable)	Area and Product	Total	In Use	Not in Use	Repair-able (Not in use	Abandoned (Not re-pairable
WORLD-Total	3222	2403	512	80	227	CARIB	879	524	140	46	169
Avgas	2047	1432	369	51	175	Avgas	747	426	135	18	158
Jet Fuel	185	185	-	-	-	Jet Fuel	36	36	-	-	-
Mogas	190	177	13	-	-	Mogas	29	25	4	-	-
Diesel	578	486	66	1	25	Diesel	34	32	1	1	-
Fuel Oil	46	46	-	-	-	Other	5	4	-	1	-
Other	56	55	-	1	-	Empty	28	1	-	26	1
Empty	120	2	64	27	27						
						EUCOM	5	5	-	-	-
OFF-SHORE-Total	3166	2351	508	80	227	Avgas	5	5	-	-	-
Avgas	1995	1400	369	51	175						
Jet Fuel	185	185	-	-	-	CINCAL	1118	826	182	11	29
Mogas	190	177	13	-	-	Avgas	504	400	89	11	4
Diesel	578	486	66	1	25	Jet Fuel	56	56	-	-	-
Fuel Oil	46	46	-	-	-	Mogas	73	65	8	-	-
Other	56	55	-	1	-	Diesel	395	305	65	-	25
Empty	116	2	60	27	27	Fuel Oil	19	19	-	-	-
						Other	50	50	-	-	-
CINCFE	428	282	145	-	1	Empty	21	1	20	-	-
Avgas	289	183	105	-	1						
Jet Fuel	61	61	-	-	-	CINCPAC	173	116	33	22	2
Mogas	34	34	-	-	-	Avgas	167	112	32	22	1
Diesel	4	4	-	-	-	Mogas	2	1	1	-	-
Empty	40	-	40	-	-	Diesel	2	2	-	-	-
						Other	1	1	-	-	-
NORLANT	563	528	8	1	26	Empty	1	-	-	-	1
Avgas	283	274	8	-	1						
Jet Fuel	32	32	-	-	-	ON-SHORE-Total	56	52	4	-	-
Mogas	52	52	-	-	-	Avgas	52	52	-	-	-
Diesel	143	143	-	-	-	Empty	4	-	4	-	-
Fuel Oil	27	27	-	-	-						
Empty	26	-	-	1	25						

Source: Armed Services Petroleum Board

FLIGHT OPERATIONS

The tables in this section provide summary data covering all phases of flight operations performed on USAF aircraft, including aircraft utilization, flying time, fuel consumption, etc. As in the case of other material presented in this edition, these tables are limited to data for the Calendar Year 1948.

As outlined in the "Introduction", preceding the tables in the Aircraft and Materiel Section of this issue, a major change was made in the type, model, series designation of USAF Aircraft, effective 1 July 1948. The required changeover has been accomplished in all Flight Operations tables affected by this classification change in the same manner and as of the same time as for applicable aircraft tables included in the Aircraft and Materiel Section. Flight data, covering the first six months of 1948, are shown in accordance with the old type, model, series designations and included in separate tabulations from similar data covering the latter half of the year which are reflected under the new designations.

Another major change affecting tables included in this section pertains to the classification of aircraft into "Active" and "Inactive" categories for flying time purposes. As in the case of the "active" and "inactive" categories for aircraft inventory use, a change was also effected in these classification concepts for flying time purposes on 1 July 1948. It was felt that, in order to depict the true utilization of USAF aircraft, the "active" concept used in an inventory sense should be further refined when used for flying time purposes. This involved elimination from the USAF "active" concept of not only those categories of aircraft considered "inactive" for inventory purposes but also those aircraft which are required to fly an appreciable amount, such as aircraft undergoing modification or depot maintenance, on projects, in repair, excess to command requirements, and aircraft grounded awaiting transfer. The resultant inventory represents the new "flying active" inventory and includes such categories as (1) aircraft being used for defense, tactical, transport and search missions, and for unit or crew training (2) those used for minimum individual training, administrative or staff work and special missions (3) aircraft used for experimental development, and test purposes (except "X" models), while those categories eliminated through its creation, as indicated above, comprise the new "non-flying active" inventory. The changeover to the new "flying" and "non-flying "active" and "inactive" categories is reflected in all flight operations tables affected thereby as of the time it occurred.

As in the case of other data included in this edition, flight tables presenting a command breakdown reflect data on "Operation Vittles" as a separate activity and consolidate the activities of the Air Defense and Tactical Air Commands into the Continental Air Command.

Data reported on Military Air Transport Service operations are for the USAF only and are shown as a separate command where applicable.

TABLE 31.-- FLYING TIME

January

	Type and Model	Total	Air Defense Command	Air Materiel Command	Air Proving Ground Command	Air Training Command	Air University	Chief of Staff
1	Total	1,705,473	80,235	141,099	4,398	344,597	55,544	10,083
2	Bomber - Total	402,796	17,089	44,591	2,322	88,794	13,410	2,253
3	B-29	115,459	-	5,917	319	3	-	-
4	B-17	52,662	384	13,019	823	4,269	173	132
5	B-25	158,394	10,499	16,691	624	80,220	7,589	1,733
6	A-26	75,249	6,206	8,358	555	4,302	5,648	388
7	Other	1,032	-	606	1	-	-	-
8	Fighter - Total	256,010	14,646	9,686	347	32,348	2,866	-
9	P-47	56,293	3,074	567	14	3	-	-
10	P-51	124,798	697	3,610	71	21,099	2,866	-
11	P-61	14,666	6,600	485	-	-	-	-
12	P-80	51,760	-	3,063	188	11,241	-	-
13	P-82	1,857	-	1,403	51	-	-	-
14	P-84	6,516	4,275	454	7	5	-	-
15	Other	120	-	104	16	-	-	-
16	Reconnaissance - Total	62,327	-	1,869	140	844	-	-
17	F-2	4,251	-	303	-	467	-	-
18	F-6	10,395	-	197	-	-	-	-
19	F-9	13,541	-	-	-	-	-	-
20	F-13	7,809	-	268	26	-	-	-
21	FA-26	9,716	-	176	-	-	-	-
22	FP-80	14,180	-	658	114	1	-	-
23	Other	2,435	-	267	-	376	-	-
24	Search & Rescue	3,119	-	42	-	-	-	-
25	Transport - Total . . .	665,843	44,731	62,915	1,247	50,351	27,518	5,955
26	C-45	112,583	19,738	17,994	311	1,017	23,277	3,076
27	C-47	355,322	24,993	40,510	891	49,190	4,241	2,879
28	C-54	143,528	-	2,280	45	132	-	-
29	C-74	1,841	-	204	-	-	-	-
30	C-82	27,311	-	491	-	-	-	-
31	C-117	3,136	-	162	-	-	-	-
32	Other	22,122	-	1,274	-	12	-	-
33	Trainer - Total . . .	272,271	3,749	19,030	313	162,009	11,693	1,848
34	AT-6	258,361	3,749	15,199	313	161,889	4,251	1,848
35	AT-7/AT-11	13,673	-	3,831	-	-	7,442	-
36	Other	237	-	-	-	120	-	-
37	Communications - Total	40,822	20	2,342	29	10,251	57	27
38	Liaison	35,392	20	1,590	21	7,839	57	27
39	Rotary Wing	5,430	-	752	8	2,412	-	-
40	Gliders and Targets . .	2,290	-	624	-	-	-	-

OF USAF AIRCRAFT BY COMMAND, TYPE AND MODEL-1948

through June 1948

Head-quarters Command	Strategic Air Command	Tactical Air Command	ATC (World-Wide)	Alaskan Air Command	AAG China	Caribbean Air Command	Far East Air Forces	JBUSMC	Pacific Air Command	US Air Forces In Europe	
59,260	215,789	180,941	218,976	38,254	3,967	44,235	207,340	1,573	25,019	74,163	1
15,302	102,327	29,369	27,041	3,913	-	6,092	40,568	309	1,944	7,472	2
-	86,532	79	13,542	873	-	-	8,178	-	16	-	3
1,649	1,116	189	8,546	2,327	-	4,752	8,593	309	1,478	4,903	4
13,653	13,613	7,468	4,821	148	-	637	698	-	-	-	5
-	641	21,633	132	565	-	703	23,099	-	450	2,569	6
-	425	-	-	-	-	-	-	-	-	-	7
2,835	51,843	30,078	-	9,584	-	7,313	66,245	-	12,266	15,953	8
-	-	7,151	-	-	-	2	17,276	-	12,266	15,940	9
2,835	36,698	12,284	-	7,113	-	-	37,512	-	-	13	10
-	-	-	-	1,379	-	818	5,384	-	-	-	11
-	14,237	9,410	-	1,055	-	6,493	6,073	-	-	-	12
-	403	-	-	-	-	-	-	-	-	-	13
-	505	1,233	-	37	-	-	-	-	-	-	14
-	-	-	-	-	-	-	-	-	-	-	15
-	11,578	23,811	143	1,978	-	3,399	16,076	-	-	2,489	16
-	1,224	-	-	108	-	448	1,701	-	-	-	17
-	-	6,620	143	-	-	11	2,291	-	-	1,133	18
-	7,604	-	-	-	-	1,659	4,278	-	-	-	19
-	2,555	-	-	1,870	-	-	3,090	-	-	-	20
-	195	7,907	-	-	-	-	82	-	-	1,356	21
-	-	9,284	-	-	-	1,281	2,842	-	-	-	22
-	-	-	-	-	-	-	1,792	-	-	-	23
-	156	-	1,650	187	-	1,079	5	-	-	-	24
38,230	42,787	67,313	184,346	18,453	3,925	22,250	41,416	1,269	7,126	46,011	25
21,342	3,543	1,761	7,585	919	-	1,437	4,589	-	1,427	4,567	26
14,362	33,214	35,576	71,845	11,879	3,587	14,937	5,551	1,269	4	40,394	27
-	6,030	3,479	100,368	4,770	338	5,806	15,592	-	4,086	602	28
-	-	-	1,637	-	-	-	-	-	-	-	29
-	-	26,497	275	48	-	-	-	-	-	-	30
2,526	-	-	-	-	-	-	-	-	-	448	31
-	-	-	2,636	837	-	70	15,684	-	1,609	-	32
2,754	7,057	19,726	1,093	2,665	-	1,881	34,079	-	2,959	1,415	33
2,754	7,057	19,726	776	582	-	1,764	34,079	-	2,959	1,415	34
-	-	-	317	2,083	-	-	-	-	-	-	35
-	-	-	-	-	-	117	-	-	-	-	36
139	41	9,396	4,703	1,462	42	2,214	8,682	-	594	823	37
139	41	8,862	4,207	974	42	1,951	8,269	-	530	823	38
-	-	534	496	488	-	263	413	-	64	-	39
-	-	1,248	-	12	-	7	269	-	130	-	40

847201 O - 49 - 5

TABLE 31.-- FLYING TIME

July through

	Type and Model	Total	Air Defense Command	Air Materiel Command	Air Proving Ground Command	Air Training Command	Air University	Chief of Staff	Continental Air Command	Head-quarters Command
1	Total	1,942,173	65,469	123,673	23,608	461,224	62,541	11,780	34,369	67,163
2	Bomber - Total	161,674	3,222	13,405	7,046	632	3,270	201	2,060	-
3	B-29	97,446	-	3,763	1,142	-	-	-	-	-
4	B-50	3,094	-	381	84	-	-	-	-	-
5	B-17	13,233	-	2,464	4,342	55	-	49	-	-
6	B-26	41,120	3,108	3,628	1,402	16	3,270	152	1,988	-
7	Other	6,781	114	3,169	76	561	-	-	72	-
8	Fighter - Total	196,907	9,516	6,961	1,652	3,586	884	-	6,838	268
9	F-47	41,943	1,006	125	72	-	-	-	951	-
10	F-51	72,910	186	3,314	352	2,586	884	-	644	268
11	F-61	9,953	2,657	430	30	3	-	-	-	-
12	F-80	48,496	-	1,818	750	985	-	-	3,147	-
13	F-82	11,479	1,649	691	260	12	-	-	804	-
14	F-84	12,030	4,018	527	148	-	-	-	1,292	-
15	Other	96	-	56	40	-	-	-	-	-
16	Reconnaissance - Total	70,407	-	1,124	738	1,506	-	2	2,328	-
17	RB-17	13,673	-	3	-	-	-	-	-	-
18	RB-29	19,490	-	177	44	-	-	-	-	-
19	RB-26	6,888	-	189	-	-	-	-	677	-
20	RF-51	6,433	-	122	-	-	-	-	441	-
21	RF-80	15,578	-	279	678	-	-	-	1,210	-
22	RC-45	4,854	-	69	-	1,098	-	2	-	-
23	Other	3,491	-	285	16	408	-	-	-	-
24	Search and Rescue	16,773	-	19	-	-	-	-	-	-
25	Transport - Total	834,129	37,984	66,996	6,955	35,427	34,216	6,664	14,252	53,542
26	C-45	116,590	16,853	13,983	1,950	1,244	28,308	3,707	3,355	24,617
27	C-47/C-117	387,428	20,516	39,789	4,816	30,879	5,297	2,799	8,321	19,936
28	C-54	237,035	-	2,187	146	120	-	-	-	-
29	C-82	29,698	-	396	43	5	-	-	1,928	-
30	CB-17	9,394	88	1,521	-	341	153	-	58	1,277
31	CB-25	23,114	256	7,279	-	1,687	382	-	459	7,712
32	CB-26	3,440	271	1,089	-	1,151	76	158	131	-
33	Other	27,430	-	752	-	-	-	-	-	-
34	Trainer - Total	619,108	14,729	32,737	6,602	410,098	24,124	4,816	7,686	13,219
35	T-6	335,772	1,771	15,879	856	245,323	437	2,783	3,350	908
36	T-7/T-11	16,169	-	4,404	-	-	9,479	-	-	-
37	TB-17	13,085	140	2,921	1,307	99	-	158	78	7
38	TB-25	161,278	9,762	5,980	2,079	102,451	8,928	1,875	1,956	10,060
39	TB-26	20,999	2,314	1,175	1,212	4,097	2,783	-	1,743	-
40	TB-29	2,709	-	497	1,120	39	-	-	-	-
41	TC-47	25,689	-	886	-	24,470	-	-	-	-
42	TF-51	32,571	742	892	-	23,120	2,497	-	547	2,244
43	TF-80	10,607	-	78	28	10,499	-	-	2	-
44	Other	229	-	25	-	-	-	-	10	-
45	Communications - Total	41,260	18	1,909	580	9,975	47	97	1,079	134
46	Liaison	34,267	18	1,180	295	6,820	47	97	904	134
47	Rotary Wing	6,993	-	729	285	3,155	-	-	175	-
48	Gliders and Targets	1,915	-	522	35	-	-	-	126	-

OF USAF AIRCRAFT BY COMMAND, TYPE AND MODEL-1948. Continued

December 1948

Strategic Air Command	Tactical Air Command	MATS World-Wide	Alaskan Air Command	AAG (China)	Caribbean Air Command	Far East Air Forces	JBUSMC	Pacific Air Command	US Air Forces in Europe	Operation Vittles	Other Overseas	
183,137	144,174	189,238	32,152	4,450	38,757	216,614	1,580	23,894	42,865	199,704	15,781	1
73,572	7,122	2,876	2,742	-	258	28,586	61	320	4,352	-	11,949	2
69,494	116	638	732	-	-	10,329	-	-	-	-	11,232	3
1,927	-	-	38	-	-	-	-	-	-	-	664	4
-	-	1,414	1,694	-	-	131	61	238	2,732	-	53	5
418	7,006	295	278	-	258	17,599	-	82	1,620	-	-	6
1,733	-	529	-	-	-	527	-	-	-	-	-	7
35,402	23,346	-	6,231	-	1,032	71,654	-	11,352	17,547	-	638	8
-	5,350	-	8	-	-	10,774	-	11,352	12,305	-	-	9
11,982	6,014	-	2,743	-	-	43,937	-	-	-	-	-	10
1	-	-	1,206	-	568	5,058	-	-	-	-	-	11
12,208	9,554	-	2,246	-	23	11,885	-	-	5,242	-	638	12
7,597	1	-	24	-	441	-	-	-	-	-	-	13
3,614	2,427	-	4	-	-	-	-	-	-	-	-	14
-	-	-	-	-	-	-	-	-	-	-	-	15
9,339	15,334	13,609	1,219	-	4,608	19,140	-	-	1,460	-	-	16
4,851	-	767	-	-	2,465	5,587	-	-	-	-	-	17
3,091	-	12,756	899	-	-	2,523	-	-	-	-	-	18
-	4,619	-	-	-	-	-	-	-	1,403	-	-	19
-	2,419	-	-	-	-	3,394	-	-	57	-	-	20
-	8,296	-	-	-	1,936	3,179	-	-	-	-	-	21
1,300	-	-	320	-	207	1,858	-	-	-	-	-	22
97	-	86	-	-	-	2,599	-	-	-	-	-	23
8	-	6,797	669	-	908	6,497	-	1,725	150	-	-	24
46,864	59,005	153,795	16,921	4,427	21,861	46,810	1,174	6,735	17,603	199,704	2,194	25
2,696	1,304	9,001	747	-	1,269	4,410	-	2,564	582	-	-	26
34,186	32,610	78,650	13,843	3,970	17,093	7,870	1,174	26	16,183	-48,824	646	27
6,190	255	58,515	1,010	457	2,363	14,963	-	848	514	149,467	-	28
8	22,257	811	289	-	-	-	-	-	-	1,413	2,548	29
629	-	659	206	-	1,079	2,515	-	668	200	-	-	30
2,802	2,139	398	-	-	-	-	-	-	-	-	-	31
-	440	-	-	-	-	-	-	-	124	-	-	32
353	-	5,761	826	-	57	17,052	-	2,629	-	-	-	33
17,892	29,179	6,942	3,125	-	7,474	35,524	329	3,191	1,443	-	-	34
6,139	16,502	731	409	-	1,454	35,085	-	2,743	1,402	-	-	35
-	-	466	1,820	-	-	-	-	-	-	-	-	36
595	194	1,118	702	-	5,398	-	329	-	39	-	-	37
9,754	3,715	4,080	194	-	5	439	-	-	-	-	-	38
509	6,264	-	-	-	454	-	-	448	-	-	-	39
894	-	159	-	-	-	-	-	-	-	-	-	40
-	-	333	-	-	-	-	-	-	-	-	-	41
1	2,473	55	-	-	-	-	-	-	-	-	-	42
-	-	-	-	-	-	-	-	-	-	-	-	43
-	31	-	-	-	163	-	-	-	-	-	-	44
60	9,342	5,219	1,228	23	2,503	8,266	16	452	312	-	-	45
60	8,711	4,289	917	23	2,107	7,923	16	414	312	-	-	46
-	631	930	311	-	396	343	-	38	-	-	-	47
-	846	-	17	-	113	127	-	119	-	-	-	48

TABLE 32.-- FLYING TIME OF USAF AIRCRAFT

Note.- In the following table all aircraft are listed under their basic type and model designator

Type and Model	Total	Jan	Feb	Mar	Apr	May	Jun
Total	3,647,651	224,506	237,991	289,087	328,546	313,687	311,661
Bomber - Total	832,241	59,478	61,274	73,773	85,516	77,737	76,442
B-17	127,457	10,576	10,371	11,232	11,324	12,002	10,698
B-25	348,338	19,559	20,535	26,026	33,303	29,556	29,791
B-26	157,412	11,424	10,963	15,040	17,009	17,396	13,133
B-29	242,913	17,826	19,314	21,340	23,657	18,561	22,570
B-50	3,975	54	80	120	212	209	206
Other	2,146	39	11	15	11	13	44
Fighter - Total	547,698	34,308	39,264	52,669	55,161	53,685	47,541
F-47	98,302	7,508	7,195	12,126	11,537	9,200	8,727
F-51	247,107	18,064	19,848	23,602	24,393	27,665	21,621
F-61	29,463	1,912	2,636	3,239	3,425	2,837	2,642
F-80	140,706	6,319	8,453	12,360	14,017	12,487	12,304
F-82	13,336	221	343	270	313	299	411
F-84	18,546	265	774	1,049	1,436	1,178	1,814
Other	238	19	15	23	40	19	22
Reconnaissance	114	-	-	-	11	0	23
Search and Rescue	7,113	401	366	296	476	901	672
Transport - Total	1,499,162	87,703	93,969	113,719	126,457	123,712	124,534
C-45	238,278	15,959	16,858	19,661	22,068	20,171	22,117
C-46	41,505	3,249	3,262	3,671	3,056	2,900	3,410
C-47/C-117	771,692	47,105	47,816	61,302	67,242	66,182	68,811
C-54	380,661	18,119	21,775	24,119	27,204	27,758	24,553
C-82	57,009	2,895	3,718	4,246	6,097	5,740	4,615
Other	10,017	376	540	720	790	961	1,028
Trainer - Total	624,375	37,084	37,654	41,975	51,910	49,997	53,651
T-6	594,133	35,513	35,534	40,119	49,711	47,169	50,315
T-7/T-11	29,842	1,493	2,041	1,829	2,191	2,807	3,312
Other	400	78	79	27	8	21	24
Communications - Total	82,843	5,194	5,221	6,342	8,818	7,495	7,752
Liaison	70,308	4,562	4,463	5,348	7,872	6,451	6,696
Rotary Wing	12,535	632	758	994	946	1,044	1,056
Gliders and Targets	4,105	338	243	113	197	160	1,039

DURING 1948, BY BASIC TYPE AND MODEL

regardless of current mission. For example: RB-29 and TB-29 are included with B-29.

Jul	Aug	Sep	Oct	Nov	Dec	Type and Model
332,852	255,146	244,725	321,559	303,676	284,215	Total
75,092	82,516	77,829	75,278	70,634	66,672	Bomber - Total
9,657	10,359	10,932	10,919	9,690	9,697	B-17
33,033	38,427	32,486	29,754	30,167	25,701	B-25
10,016	11,579	13,327	14,259	11,674	11,592	B-26
22,003	21,474	20,184	19,797	18,294	17,893	B-29
194	320	364	294	649	1,273	B-50
189	357	536	255	160	516	Other
45,913	49,223	47,056	41,572	42,902	38,404	Fighter - Total
7,943	8,361	8,231	6,752	5,576	5,146	F-47
19,610	20,151	18,993	17,319	19,226	16,615	F-51
2,356	2,709	2,518	2,172	1,657	1,360	F-61
12,156	13,221	13,820	11,688	12,576	11,305	F-80
1,037	1,502	1,128	2,602	2,669	2,541	F-82
2,735	3,270	2,350	1,028	1,185	1,412	F-84
26	9	16	11	13	25	Other
5	8	40	6	2	19	Reconnaissance - Total
498	544	741	905	630	676	Search and Rescue
146,431	149,293	149,037	141,060	119,153	124,094	Transport - Total
21,111	22,361	21,306	21,117	17,608	17,881	C-45
3,492	3,682	3,169	3,794	3,308	4,012	C-46
81,467	77,795	76,328	65,057	55,814	56,773	C-47/C-117
34,258	38,593	41,027	45,585	36,872	40,798	C-54
5,177	5,660	6,226	4,780	4,403	3,452	C-82
926	1,202	921	727	648	1,178	Other
57,009	65,568	62,869	55,122	52,964	48,572	Trainer - Total
53,700	62,806	60,028	52,137	60,313	46,790	T-6
3,272	2,724	2,817	2,966	2,611	1,779	T-7/T-11
37	38	26	19	40	3	Other
7,635	7,597	6,835	7,357	7,038	5,559	Communications - Total
6,818	6,372	5,470	5,948	5,794	4,514	Liaison
817	1,225	1,365	1,409	1,244	1,045	Rotary Wing
269	397	318	259	353	219	Gliders and Targets

TABLE 33.-- USAF FLYING TIME IN CONTINENTAL U.S., BY TYPE AND MODEL: DURING 1948

(Excluding Air Transport Command and Air Reserve)

Type and Model	Total Jan-Jun	Jan	Feb	Mar	Apr	May	Jun
Total	1,091,946	141,083	148,072	179,191	215,329	203,107	205,164
Bomber - Total	315,457	43,876	43,989	52,219	61,962	55,660	57,751
B-29	92,850	15,297	14,951	16,159	15,973	12,575	17,895
B-17	21,754	4,346	4,018	3,340	3,329	3,691	3,030
B-25	152,090	18,497	19,506	24,646	32,111	28,613	28,717
A-26	47,731	5,642	5,421	7,937	10,319	10,557	7,855
Other	1,032	94	93	137	230	224	254
Fighter - Total	144,649	15,970	20,215	26,227	29,158	28,076	25,003
F-47	10,809	1,597	1,344	2,665	1,796	1,687	1,720
F-51	80,160	9,908	11,557	13,356	15,596	16,809	12,934
F-61	7,085	677	1,246	1,544	1,412	1,011	1,195
F-80	38,139	3,284	4,955	7,342	8,572	7,075	6,911
F-82	1,857	221	343	270	313	299	411
F-84	6,479	265	757	1,029	1,436	1,178	1,814
Other	120	18	13	21	33	17	18
Reconnaissance - Total	34,243	4,579	4,598	6,514	8,156	7,596	6,490
F-2	1,994	185	228	294	429	332	526
F-6	6,817	461	505	1,077	1,642	1,735	1,397
F-9	5,720	429	294	375	1,737	1,585	1,320
F-13	2,849	317	375	481	488	665	523
FB-17	1,864	543	513	808	-	-	-
F-26	8,278	1,211	1,231	1,484	1,799	1,641	912
FP-80	10,057	1,353	1,268	1,922	1,927	1,797	1,690
Other	643	80	84	73	134	141	131
Search and Rescue	198	21	20	8	50	59	40
Transport - Total	341,047	43,968	46,484	56,607	65,601	64,185	64,202
C-45	92,059	12,230	12,956	15,494	17,528	16,078	17,773
C-47/117	208,544	27,799	27,682	34,917	38,959	39,427	39,760
C-54	11,966	790	1,822	1,801	2,764	2,813	1,976
C-74	204	14	36	35	71	19	29
C-82	26,988	2,893	3,717	4,133	6,055	5,648	4,542
Other	1,286	242	271	227	224	200	122
Trainer - Total	228,179	30,094	30,317	34,017	44,954	42,437	46,360
AT-6	216,786	28,722	28,541	32,560	43,198	40,100	43,665
AT-7/AT-11	11,273	1,322	1,717	1,446	1,756	2,337	2,695
Other	120	50	59	11	-	-	-
Communications - Total	22,302	2,301	2,296	3,379	5,293	4,674	4,359
Liaison	18,596	1,837	1,766	2,670	4,781	3,965	3,577
Rotary Wing	3,706	464	530	709	512	709	782
Gliders and Targets	1,872	274	153	220	155	120	950

TABLE 33.-- USAF FLYING TIME IN CONTINENTAL U.S., BY TYPE AND MODEL: DURING 1948. Continued

(Excluding Military Air Transport Service and Air Reserve)

Type and Model	Total Jul-Dec	Jul	Aug	Sep	Oct	Nov	Dec
Total	1,177,138	205,107	225,643	209,665	190,054	183,641	163,028
Bomber - Total	110,530	20,147	20,352	21,870	18,018	13,614	16,529
B-36	1,255	114	172	305	69	107	488
B-29	74,515	16,091	15,330	14,199	10,571	8,048	10,276
B-50	2,392	194	320	364	294	493	727
B-17	6,910	1,282	1,088	1,249	1,322	933	1,036
B-26	20,988	1,927	2,691	4,875	4,962	3,143	3,390
Other	4,470	539	751	878	800	890	612
Fighter - Total	88,453	18,223	17,840	15,628	13,327	11,517	11,918
F-47	7,504	1,375	1,454	1,642	1,146	908	979
F-51	26,230	6,126	5,147	4,744	3,906	2,824	3,483
F-61	3,121	1,177	982	584	332	29	17
F-80	28,462	5,697	5,476	5,164	4,462	4,003	3,660
F-82	11,014	1,037	1,502	1,128	2,442	2,555	2,350
F-84	12,026	2,785	3,270	2,350	1,028	1,185	1,408
Other	96	26	9	16	11	13	21
Reconnaissance - Total	30,371	5,043	5,897	5,555	5,073	4,430	4,373
RB-17	4,854	485	700	1,135	880	742	912
RB-29	3,312	635	464	428	618	507	660
RB-26	5,485	722	1,306	1,067	920	745	725
RF-51	2,982	779	436	535	422	352	458
RF-80	10,463	1,830	2,385	1,744	1,496	1,714	1,294
RC-45	2,469	482	522	525	494	239	207
Other	806	110	84	121	243	131	117
Search and Rescue	27	10	3	-	6	8	-
Transport - Total	361,905	64,463	67,161	62,865	62,387	53,030	51,999
C-45	98,017	16,818	18,691	17,161	16,916	13,938	14,493
C-47/C-117	199,149	35,580	36,504	33,657	34,937	29,288	29,183
C-54	8,898	1,938	1,543	1,263	1,517	1,544	1,093
C-82	24,637	5,062	5,461	5,460	3,472	3,188	1,994
CB-17	4,067	681	531	603	657	535	1,060
CB-25	22,716	3,797	3,718	3,881	4,099	3,765	3,456
CB-26	3,316	394	512	719	626	568	497
Other	1,105	193	201	121	163	204	223
Trainer - Total	561,082	92,857	109,825	99,723	86,834	96,837	75,006
T-6	293,948	47,576	56,999	53,201	44,426	52,930	38,816
T-7/T-11	13,883	2,864	2,255	2,360	2,627	2,259	1,518
TB-17	5,499	1,012	1,057	931	1,110	763	626
TB-25	156,560	27,686	32,936	26,826	23,866	24,541	20,705
TB-26	20,097	2,540	3,327	3,572	4,088	3,042	3,528
TB-29	2,550	474	445	452	443	460	276
TC-47	25,356	4,315	4,722	4,473	4,369	4,199	3,278
TF-51	32,516	4,701	6,645	5,649	4,366	6,713	4,442
TF-80	10,607	1,671	1,433	2,236	1,531	1,929	1,807
Other	66	18	6	23	8	1	10
Communications - Total	23,241	4,138	4,225	3,794	4,238	3,869	2,977
Liaison	18,266	3,511	3,412	2,821	3,249	2,974	2,299
Rotary Wing	4,975	627	813	973	989	895	678
Gliders and Targets	1,529	226	340	230	171	336	226

TABLE 34. -- USAF FLYING TIME OVERSEAS, BY TYPE AND MODEL: DURING 1948

(Excluding Air Transport Command)

Type and Model	Total Jan-Jun	Jan	Feb	Mar	Apr	May	Jun
Total	394,556	55,369	57,314	73,289	72,092	69,102	67,390
Bomber - Total	60,298	8,695	8,730	11,556	11,769	10,161	9,387
B-29	9,067	990	886	1,784	3,191	1,004	1,212
B-17	22,362	3,174	3,328	4,051	3,859	4,086	3,864
B-25	1,483	274	358	398	103	130	220
A-26	27,386	4,257	4,158	5,323	4,616	4,941	4,091
Fighter - Total	111,361	14,873	15,819	21,690	20,821	20,367	17,791
P-47	45,484	5,911	5,851	9,461	9,741	7,513	7,007
P-51	44,638	7,048	7,285	8,451	6,693	8,479	6,682
P-61	7,581	923	1,161	1,439	1,592	1,407	1,059
P-80	13,621	991	1,505	2,319	2,795	2,968	3,043
P-84	37	-	17	20	-	-	-
Reconnaissance - Total	23,942	3,413	3,307	4,623	4,149	4,155	4,295
F-2	2,257	222	472	483	330	308	442
F-6	3,435	611	484	705	421	629	585
F-9	3,501	182	246	235	866	932	1,040
F-13	4,960	553	413	761	1,153	1,062	1,018
FB-17	2,436	571	727	1,138	-	-	-
FA-26	1,438	314	153	296	275	203	197
FP-80	4,123	691	625	777	723	647	660
Other	1,792	269	187	228	381	374	353
Search and Rescue	1,271	218	176	131	274	223	249
Transport - Total	140,450	19,290	20,067	25,202	25,421	24,513	25,957
C-45	12,939	2,267	2,039	2,109	2,340	2,042	2,142
C-46	17,517	2,910	2,899	3,328	2,689	2,565	3,126
C-47/C-117	78,069	9,585	10,241	14,258	14,892	13,736	15,357
C-54	31,194	4,401	4,789	5,369	5,450	6,015	5,172
Other	731	127	101	138	50	155	160
Trainer - Total	42,999	6,873	7,147	7,771	6,766	7,382	7,060
AT-6	40,799	6,674	6,866	7,451	6,372	6,962	6,474
AT-7/AT-11	2,083	171	261	304	386	399	562
Other	117	28	20	16	8	21	24
Communications - Total	13,817	1,943	1,978	2,223	2,850	2,261	2,562
Liaison	12,589	1,841	1,841	2,027	2,532	2,026	2,322
Rotary Wing	1,228	102	137	196	318	235	240
Gliders and Targets	418	64	90	93	42	40	89

TABLE 34.-- USAF FLYING TIME OVERSEAS, BY TYPE AND MODEL: DURING 1948, Continued

(Excluding Military Air Transport Service)

Type and Model	Total Jul-Dec	Jul	Aug	Sep	Oct	Nov	Dec
Total	376,093	56,967	61,182	62,010	66,554	67,387	61,993
Bomber - Total	48,258	6,797	6,390	5,689	9,327	11,601	8,464
B-29	22,293	1,898	2,070	2,039	5,297	6,949	4,040
B-17	4,909	1,026	975	960	765	593	590
B-26	19,837	3,826	3,258	2,581	3,158	3,795	3,219
Other	1,229	47	87	109	107	264	615
Fighter - Total	108,454	17,223	18,730	19,360	18,276	18,600	16,265
F-47	34,439	6,550	6,901	6,566	5,598	4,667	4,157
F-51	46,680	7,412	7,271	7,415	7,972	8,840	7,770
F-61	6,832	901	1,189	1,490	1,413	1,026	813
F-80	20,034	2,360	3,369	3,389	3,133	3,953	3,330
Other	469	-	-	-	160	114	195
Reconnaissance - Total	26,427	3,974	4,056	4,401	4,789	4,500	4,707
RB-17	8,052	1,144	1,117	1,411	1,487	1,365	1,528
RB-29	3,422	635	688	586	566	434	513
RB-26	1,403	431	251	285	230	151	55
RF-51	3,451	578	652	627	635	497	462
RF-61	2,599	245	512	435	293	585	529
RF-80	5,115	578	534	776	1,060	965	1,202
RC-45	2,385	363	302	281	518	503	418
Search and Rescue	9,508	1,226	2,162	1,684	1,440	1,603	1,393
Transport - Total	118,725	17,577	19,835	20,164	21,143	19,920	20,086
C-45	9,572	1,751	1,715	1,643	1,632	1,358	1,473
C-46	19,851	3,145	3,200	2,878	3,493	3,520	3,615
C-47/C-117	60,805	8,484	9,168	9,839	11,270	10,777	11,267
C-54	20,155	3,324	4,771	4,682	2,774	2,670	1,934
C-82	2,837	53	58	23	854	738	1,111
CB-17	4,668	585	726	939	980	790	648
CB-26	124	-	-	-	60	54	10
Other	713	235	197	160	80	13	28
Trainer - Total	51,084	7,650	7,441	8,394	9,367	8,904	9,328
T-6	41,093	6,021	5,671	6,651	7,575	7,264	7,911
T-7/11	1,820	361	390	387	253	233	196
TB-17	6,468	1,031	1,039	1,011	1,256	1,160	971
TB-25	638	116	90	146	99	79	108
TB-26	902	84	213	173	165	128	139
Other	163	37	38	26	19	40	3
Communication - Total	13,241	2,457	2,487	2,219	2,118	2,230	1,730
Liaison	12,078	2,315	2,231	1,999	1,900	2,067	1,566
Rotary Wing	1,163	142	256	220	218	163	164
Gliders and Targets	386	63	81	99	94	29	20

TABLE 35.-- USAF FLYING TIME IN AIR TRANSPORT COMMAND, BY TYPE AND MODEL JAN THROUGH JUN 1948

Type and Model	Total	Jan	Feb	Mar	Apr	May	June
Total	218,976	28,054	32,605	36,607	41,125	41,478	39,107
Bomber - Total	27,041	2,751	4,563	4,377	5,391	5,734	4,225
B-29	13,542	669	2,689	2,155	2,852	3,255	1,922
B-17	8,546	1,331	1,245	1,285	1,533	1,708	1,444
B-25	4,821	751	629	937	1,006	717	781
Other	132	-	-	-	-	54	78
Reconnaissance	143	36	17	13	41	13	23
Search and Rescue	1,650	162	170	157	152	619	390
Transport - Total	184,346	24,038	26,718	31,133	34,676	34,374	33,407
C-45	7,585	1,055	1,163	1,281	1,441	1,411	1,234
C-46	976	119	166	179	148	166	198
C-47	71,845	9,721	9,893	12,127	13,391	13,019	13,694
C-54	100,366	12,928	15,166	16,949	18,990	18,930	17,405
C-74	1,637	102	109	209	371	386	460
C-97	1,376	72	195	251	277	291	290
Other	559	41	26	137	58	171	126
Trainer - Total	1,093	117	190	187	190	178	231
AT-6	776	117	127	108	141	107	176
AT-7/11	317	-	63	79	49	71	55
Communications - Total	4,703	950	947	740	675	560	831
Liaison	4,207	884	856	651	559	460	797
Rotary Wing	496	66	91	89	116	100	34

TABLE 36.-- USAF FLYING TIME IN MILITARY AIR TRANSPORT SERVICE, BY TYPE AND MODEL
JUL THROUGH DEC 1948

Type and Model	Total	Jul	Aug	Sep	Oct	Nov	Dec
Total	189,238	39,995	32,174	31,749	30,337	27,326	27,657
Bomber - Total	2,876	904	675	404	351	221	321
B-29	638	314	111	28	54	30	101
B-17	1,414	362	335	253	225	81	158
B-25	529	136	208	68	22	62	33
B-26	295	92	21	55	50	48	29
Reconnaissance - Total	13,609	2,194	2,492	2,487	2,310	1,974	2,152
RB-17	767	205	83	72	118	114	175
RB-29	12,756	1,956	2,356	2,415	2,192	1,860	1,977
RC-47	86	33	53	-	-	-	-
Search and Rescue	6,797	705	792	1,168	1,467	1,437	1,228
Transport - Total	153,795	34,071	26,214	25,735	24,027	21,620	22,128
C-45	9,001	1,697	1,131	1,756	1,557	1,570	1,290
C-46	1,304	189	342	179	206	166	222
C-47	78,650	13,699	13,702	13,372	13,524	11,426	12,927
C-54	58,515	17,569	9,778	9,247	7,914	7,611	6,396
C-74	2,995	344	434	343	481	510	883
C-82	811	62	141	192	91	164	161
C-97	992	239	441	259	-	-	53
Other	1,527	272	245	387	254	173	196
Trainer - Total	6,942	1,081	1,225	1,178	1,268	1,186	1,004
T-6	731	103	136	174	136	119	63
T-11	466	47	79	70	86	119	65
TB-17	1,118	202	291	192	148	181	104
TB-25	4,080	715	709	610	776	649	621
Other	547	14	10	132	122	118	151
Communications - Total	5,219	1,040	776	777	914	888	824
Liaison	4,289	992	637	619	718	702	621
Rotary Wing	930	48	139	158	196	186	203

TABLE 37.-- UTILIZATION AND MAINTENANCE

	Month	Air Defense Command	Air Materiel Command	Air Proving Ground Command	Air Training Command	Air University	Chief of Staff	Continental Air Command	Head-quarters Command
	Jan a/								
1	Hours Flown	9,705	19,415	c/	44,883	6,788	925	-	8,212
2	Average Aircraft on Hand	433	1,038	-	1,140	336	32	-	179
3	Average Aircraft in Commission	242	562	-	750	238	20	-	146
4	Av. Hrs. Flown Per A/C On Hand	22	19	-	59	20	29	-	46
	Feb a/								
5	Hours Flown	11,503	19,055	c/	43,793	8,065	1,286	-	8,808
6	Average Aircraft On Hand	421	1,039	-	1,125	333	67	-	171
7	Average Aircraft in Commission	244	566	-	736	238	50	-	140
8	Av. Hrs. Flown Per A/C On Hand	27	18	-	39	24	19	-	52
	Mar a/								
9	Hours Flown	14,333	23,153	c/	50,590	9,522	1,726	-	9,718
10	Average Aircraft On Hand	437	901	-	1,161	332	83	-	167
11	Average Aircraft in Commission	272	503	-	781	221	58	-	138
12	Av. Hrs. Flown Per A/C On Hand	33	26	-	44	29	21	-	58
	Apr a/								
13	Hours Flown	15,148	26,469	c/	72,922	9,958	1,975	-	10,877
14	Average Aircraft On Hand	453	878	-	1,241	285	78	-	172
15	Average Aircraft in Commission	298	525	-	827	187	58	-	141
16	Av. Hrs. Flown Per A/C On Hand	33	30	-	59	35	25	-	63
	May a/								
17	Hours Flown	14,082	25,436	c/	65,101	10,467	2,063	-	10,743
18	Average Aircraft On Hand	437	873	-	1,362	265	77	-	166
19	Average Aircraft in Commission	286	492	-	963	166	60	-	134
20	Av. Hrs. Flown Per A/C On Hand	32	29	-	48	39	27	-	65
	Jun a/								
21	Hours Flown	15,457	20,844	4,396	66,997	10,367	2,103	-	10,893
22	Average Aircraft On Hand	422	705	172	1,452	271	79	-	168
23	Average Aircraft in Commission	259	373	104	972	166	56	-	131
24	Av. Hrs. Flown Per A/C On Hand	37	30	26	46	38	27	-	65
	Jul b/								
25	Hours Flown	14,968	21,501	4,405	72,401	10,207	1,946	-	10,560
26	Average Aircraft On Hand	414	948	183	1,467	279	73	-	171
27	Average Aircraft in Commission	237	392	84	1,045	184	51	-	138
28	Av. Hrs. Flown Per A/C On Hand	36	23	24	49	37	27	-	62
	Aug b/								
29	Hours Flown	15,316	22,721	4,040	83,790	10,832	2,456	-	11,955
30	Average Aircraft On Hand	410	890	184	1,451	281	82	-	174
31	Average Aircraft in Commission	249	391	89	1,064	198	64	-	144
32	Av. Hrs. Flown Per A/C On Hand	37	26	22	61	39	30	-	69
	Sep b/								
33	Hours Flown	12,758	19,749	4,235	82,089	11,360	2,215	-	11,491
34	Average Aircraft On Hand	414	859	186	1,459	286	77	-	176
35	Average Aircraft in Commission	243	397	87	1,095	204	57	-	145
36	Av. Hrs. Flown Per A/C On Hand	31	22	23	56	40	29	-	65
	Oct b/								
37	Hours Flown	12,166	20,665	4,121	70,101	12,056	1,907	-	11,858
38	Average Aircraft On Hand	437	820	171	1,523	283	72	-	179
39	Average Aircraft in Commission	259	393	84	1,058	193	55	-	148
40	Av. Hrs. Flown Per A/C On Hand	28	25	24	46	43	26	-	66
	Nov b/								
41	Hours Flown	10,242	17,454	3,259	84,824	9,680	1,602	-	10,740
42	Average Aircraft On Hand	412	824	167	1,639	285	73	-	178
43	Average Aircraft in Commission	236	398	92	1,139	190	55	-	150
44	Av. Hrs. Flown Per A/C On Hand	25	21	20	52	34	22	-	60
	Dec b/								
45	Hours Flown	-	17,197	3,476	63,019	8,406	1,654	33,900	10,539
46	Average Aircraft On Hand	-	804	158	1,737	282	75	1,723	174
47	Average Aircraft in Commission	-	393	76	1,225	139	57	828	137
48	Av. Hrs. Flown Per A/C On Hand	-	21	22	36	30	22	20	61

a/ During the period 1 Jan-30 Jun aircraft in the following categories were excluded: storage, excess, bailment.

b/ Due to a revision of the flying active inventory (effective 1 July 1948), in addition to above, air-the year.

c/ Included with Air Materiel Command

OF USAF AIRCRAFT, BY COMMAND-MONTHLY 1948

Strategic Air Command	Tactical Air Command	MATS World-Wide	Alaskan Air Command	AAG (China)	Caribbean Air Command	Far East Air Forces	JBUSMC	Pacific Air Command	US Air Forces in Europe	Other Overseas	Operation Vittles	
28,998	20,831	28,028	4,749	619	5,726	31,700	296	3,506	8,265	-	-	1
865	1,194	606	220	30	296	1,312	5	161	374	-	-	2
517	653	328	101	21	133	650	2	78	244	-	-	3
34	17	46	22	21	19	24	59	22	22	-	-	4
33,489	20,723	32,600	5,013	622	6,037	31,777	263	3,991	9,095	-	-	5
877	1,210	658	235	29	306	1,304	5	162	378	-	-	6
525	642	384	99	22	159	643	2	65	229	-	-	7
38	17	50	21	21	20	24	53	25	24	-	-	8
36,335	32,062	36,584	6,203	809	7,268	39,221	308	4,117	14,910	-	-	9
896	1,220	629	244	29	325	1,313	3	155	362	-	-	10
544	638	358	108	22	165	686	2	79	230	-	-	11
41	26	58	25	28	22	30	102	27	41	-	-	12
39,986	36,626	41,059	6,750	709	8,414	35,758	272	4,232	15,710	-	-	13
899	1,209	632	241	31	326	1,347	4	152	362	-	-	14
567	670	383	123	27	171	723	4	77	259	-	-	15
44	30	65	28	23	26	27	68	28	43	-	-	16
36,467	37,311	41,470	6,866	617	8,043	35,510	195	4,466	12,641	-	-	17
863	1,238	648	244	31	309	1,324	3	156	352	-	-	18
562	734	398	126	27	175	697	3	84	231	-	-	19
42	30	64	28	20	26	27	65	29	36	-	-	20
39,835	33,031	39,079	8,555	591	8,614	31,764	244	4,571	12,718	-	-	21
907	1,254	648	256	30	320	1,308	3	157	358	-	-	22
586	669	375	147	23	195	680	3	93	244	-	-	23
44	26	60	33	20	27	24	81	29	36	-	-	24
26,936	31,125	39,995	6,585	758	6,223	33,367	301	3,997	5,517	-	30,764	25
1,025	1,276	635	258	31	252	1,457	4	161	454	-	177	26
653	627	354	141	21	128	774	3	104	170	•	128	27
36	24	63	26	24	25	23	75	25	12	-	174	28
35,431	33,196	32,174	7,283	682	6,310	34,642	256	4,940	6,797	-	36,147	29
1,137	1,259	573	254	30	247	1,492	4	157	316	-	226	30
644	599	343	140	20	119	673	2	91	184	-	149	31
31	26	56	29	23	26	23	64	31	22	-	160	32
33,395	31,621	31,749	5,724	623	6,911	36,139	216	4,091	7,811	-	41,301	33
1,200	1,240	560	254	26	238	1,479	4	160	300	-	215	34
681	663	328	106	19	130	646	3	94	195	-	135	35
28	26	57	23	24	29	24	54	26	26	-	192	36
29,370	26,216	30,328	4,845	781	7,041	37,001	278	4,154	7,663	4,397	34,614	37
1,095	1,122	535	248	26	248	1,410	5	152	356	107	172	38
577	607	309	117	16	137	665	3	83	213	83	109	39
27	23	57	20	30	28	26	56	27	22	41	201	40
24,190	19,684	27,314	3,767	983	6,067	38,450	189	3,397	7,637	6,701	25,322	41
1,050	1,064	527	254	27	245	1,331	5	158	406	193	160	42
562	579	298	99	22	142	760	3	72	247	143	95	43
23	19	52	15	36	25	28	38	22	19	35	158	44
23,758	-	27,651	3,948	623	6,204	36,990	324	3,315	5,898	4,683	31,537	45
873	-	503	247	23	228	1,354	4	146	376	155	181	46
451	-	281	106	20	127	714	4	77	255	114	101	47
26	-	55	16	27	27	27	81	23	16	30	174	48

grounded pending transfer, reclamation salvage or survey, depot maintenance, modification, project, and craft on loan to a Non-USAF organization, and all "X" models were excluded during the last six months of

TABLE 38.-- UTILIZATION AND MAINTENANCE OF USAF AIRCRAFT, BY TYPE AND MODEL AND BY TYPE OF FLYING: DURING 1948

Note:-- The data below is designed to reflect aircraft maintenance and utilization by type of activity and is based on the "Flying Active" aircraft inventory only. The various types of flying activity are defined in the Glossary.

January through June 1948

Type of Flying		Total USAF	Bomber				
			B-29	B-17	B-25	A-26	Other
ADMINIS-TRATIVE	Hours Flown	20,163	-	1,640	750	-	-
	Average Aircraft On Hand	71	-	4	4	-	-
	Average Aircraft In Commission	60	-	4	4	-	-
	Av. Hrs. Flown Per A/C On Hand	47	-	68	31	-	-
MINIMUM INDI-VIDUAL TRAINING	Hours Flown	660,981	1,444	23,564	112,613	33,552	-
	Average Aircraft On Hand	2,793	6	96	451	191	-
	Average Aircraft In Commission	1,795	2	73	269	106	-
	Av. Hrs. Flown Per A/C On Hand	39	40	41	42	29	-
OPERA-TIONAL	Hours Flown	967,230	103,773	20,629	42,274	39,215	356
	Average Aircraft On Hand	4,709	369	100	126	195	2
	Average Aircraft In Commission	2,795	208	68	76	88	1
	Av. Hrs. Flown Per A/C On Hand	34	47	34	56	34	30
RESEARCH AND DEVELOP-MENT a/	Hours Flown	40,244	7,971	5,750	2,308	1,760	564
	Average Aircraft On Hand	508	67	47	22	27	15
	Average Aircraft In Commission	253	34	25	13	12	3
	Av. Hrs. Flown Per A/C On Hand	13	20	20	18	11	6
TOTAL FLYING ACTIVE	Hours Flown	1,688,618	113,188	51,583	157,945	74,527	920
	Average Aircraft On Hand	8,081	442	247	603	413	17
	Average Aircraft In Commission	4,903	244	170	362	206	4
	Av. Hrs. Flown Per A/C On Hand	35	43	35	44	30	9
	All Other Flying Time	16,860	2,271	1,079	449	722	112
	Grand Total Hours Flown	1,705,478	115,459	52,662	158,394	75,249	1,032

Type of Flying		Fighter					
		P-47	P-51	P-61	P-80	P-82	P-84	Other
ADMINIS-TRATIVE	Hours Flown	-	-	-	-	-	-	-
	Average Aircraft On Hand	-	-	-	-	-	-	-
	Average Aircraft In Commission	-	-	-	-	-	-	-
	Av. Hrs. Flown Per A/C On Hand	-	-	-	-	-	-	-
MINIMUM INDI-VIDUAL TRAINING	Hours Flown	1,181	10,741	145	5,074	-	-	-
	Average Aircraft On Hand	14	79	1	48	-	-	-
	Average Aircraft In Commission	5	44	-	27	-	-	-
	Av. Hrs. Flown Per A/C On Hand	14	23	24	18	-	-	-
OPERA-TIONAL	Hours Flown	53,718	110,859	13,909	43,620	202	6,011	-
	Average Aircraft On Hand	408	773	97	362	1	119	-
	Average Aircraft In Commission	217	456	44	207	-	48	-
	Av. Hrs. Flown Per A/C On Hand	22	24	24	120	34	8	-
RESEARCH AND DEVELOP-MENT a/	Hours Flown	314	1,222	480	2,620	1,651	496	120
	Average Aircraft On Hand	12	21	11	56	22	25	7
	Average Aircraft In Commission	6	12	5	27	10	7	4
	Av. Hrs. Flown Per A/C On Hand	4	10	7	8	13	3	3
TOTAL FLYING ACTIVE	Hours Flown	55,213	122,822	14,534	51,314	1,853	6,509	120
	Average Aircraft On Hand	434	873	109	466	23	144	7
	Average Aircraft In Commission	228	512	49	261	10	55	4
	Av. Hrs. Flown Per A/C On Hand	21	23	22	18	13	8	3
	All Other Flying Time	1,080	1,976	132	446	4	7	-
	Total Hours Flown	56,293	124,798	14,666	51,760	1,857	6,516	120

a/ Experimental or "X" models are included in Research and Development category January through June.

TABLE 38.— UTILIZATION AND MAINTENANCE OF USAF AIRCRAFT, BY TYPE, AND MODEL AND BY TYPE OF FLYING: DURING 1948, Continued

January through June 1948

Type of Flying		Reconnaissance							Search And Rescue
		F-2	F-6	F-9	F-13	FA-26	FP-80	Other	
ADMINIS- TRATIVE	Hours Flown	-	-	-	-	-	-	-	-
	Average Aircraft On Hand	-	-	-	-	-	-	-	-
	Average Aircraft In Commission	-	-	-	-	-	-	-	-
	Av. Hrs. Flown Per A/C On Hand	-	-	-	-	-	-	-	-
MINIMUM INDI- VIDUAL TRAINING	Hours Flown	966	623	469	26	-	-	-	-
	Average Aircraft On Hand	4	5	2	1	-	-	-	-
	Average Aircraft In Commission	3	4	1	-	-	-	-	-
	Av. Hrs. Flown Per A/C On Hand	40	21	39	4	-	-	-	-
OPERA- TIONAL	Hours Flown	2,982	9,603	13,070	7,462	9,540	13,388	2,155	3,068
	Average Aircraft On Hand	22	63	63	27	46	86	18	23
	Average Aircraft In Commission	15	31	38	13	32	63	12	15
	Av. Hrs. Flown Per A/C On Hand	23	25	35	46	35	26	20	22
RESEARCH AND DEVELOP- MENT a/	Hours Flown	170	118	-	238	174	677	266	-
	Average Aircraft On Hand	1	1	-	2	2	8	4	-
	Average Aircraft In Commission	1	1	-	2	2	7	1	-
	Av. Hrs. Flown Per A/C On Hand	28	20	-	20	15	14	11	-
TOTAL FLYING ACTIVE	Hours Flown	4,118	10,344	13,539	7,726	9,714	14,065	2,421	3,068
	Average Aircraft On Hand	27	69	65	30	48	94	22	23
	Average Aircraft In Commission	19	36	39	15	34	70	13	15
	Av. Hrs. Flown Per A/C On Hand	25	25	35	43	34	25	18	22
	All Other Flying Time	133	51	2	83	2	115	14	51
	Total Hours Flown	4,251	10,395	13,541	7,809	9,716	14,180	2,435	3,119

Type of Flying		Transport					
		C-45	C-46	C-47/117	C-54	C-82	Other
ADMINIS- TRATIVE	Hours Flown	-	-	14,767	2,867	-	139
	Average Aircraft On Hand	-	-	55	7	-	1
	Average Aircraft In Commission	-	-	46	6	-	-
	Av. Hrs. Flown Per A/C On Hand	-	-	45	68	-	23
MINIMUM INDI- VIDUAL TRAINING	Hours Flown	108,131	3,571	210,051	8,531	55	61
	Average Aircraft On Hand	409	17	640	24	2	4
	Average Aircraft In Commission	283	8	430	13	-	.1
	Av. Hrs. Flown Per A/C On Hand	44	35	55	59	5	4
OPERA- TIONAL	Hours Flown	2,879	15,001	125,351	129,586	26,679	2,248
	Average Aircraft On Hand	20	78	397	266	142	11
	Average Aircraft In Commission	12	34	265	139	69	7
	Av. Hrs. Flown Per A/C On Hand	24	32	53	81	31	34
RESEARCH AND DEVELOP- MENT a/	Hours Flown	1,091	534	4,104	1,668	462	1,783
	Average Aircraft On Hand	12	3	37	14	6	9
	Average Aircraft In Commission	10	2	15	6	4	3
	Av. Hrs. Flown Per A/C On Hand	15	30	18	20	13	33
TOTAL FLYING ACTIVE	Hours Flown	112,101	19,106	354,273	142,652	27,196	4,251
	Average Aircraft On Hand	441	98	1,129	311	150	25
	Average Aircraft In Commission	305	44	756	164	73	11
	Av. Hrs. Flown Per A/C On Hand	42	32	52	76	30	28
	All Other Flying Time	482	442	4,185	876	115	164
	Total Hours Flown	112,583	19,548	358,458	143,528	27,311	4,415

a/ Flying time of "R" models are included in "All Other Flying" July through December

TABLE 38.-- UTILIZATION AND MAINTENCE OF USAF AIRCRAFT, BY TYPE AND MODEL AND BY TYPE OF FLYING: DURING 1948.Continued

January through June 1948

Type of Flying		Trainer			Communications		Gliders and Targets
		AT-6	AT-7/11	Other	Liaison	Rotary Wing	
ADMINIS-TRATIVE	Hours Flown Average Aircraft On Hand Average Aircraft In Commission Av. Hrs. Flown Per A/C On Hand	- - - -	- - - -	- - - -	- - - -	- - - -	- - - -
MINIMUM INDI-VIDUAL TRAINING	Hours Flown Average Aircraft On Hand Average Aircraft In Commission Av. Hrs. Flown Per A/C On Hand	119,778 636 415 31	12,154 64 47 32	137 4 2 6	7,850 77 48 17	198 6 3 6	46 12 11 1
OPERA-TIONAL	Hours Flown Average Aircraft On Hand Average Aircraft In Commission Av. Hrs. Flown Per A/C On Hand	137,236 449 343 51	829 5 3 28	- - - -	25,426 167 132 25	4,572 74 32 10	1,589 200 127 1
RESEARCH AND DEVELOP-MENT a/	Hours Flown Average Aircraft On Hand Average Aircraft In Commission Av. Hrs. Flown Per A/C On Hand	719 6 4 20	344 5 4 11	- - - -	1,396 24 13 10	624 15 6 7	618 27 14 4
TOTAL FLYING ACTIVE	Hours Flown Average Aircraft On Hand Average Aircraft In Commission Av. Hrs. Flown Per A/C On Hand	257,733 1,091 762 39	13,327 74 54 30	137 4 2 6	34,672 268 193 22	5,394 95 41 9	2,253 239 152 2
	All Other Flying Time	628	346	100	720	36	37
	Total Hours Flown	258,361	13,673	237	35,392	5,430	2,290

TABLE 38.-- UTILIZATION AND MAINTENANCE OF USAF AIRCRAFT, BY TYPE AND MODEL AND BY TYPE OF FLYING: DURING 1948.Continued

July through December 1948

Type of Flying		Total USAF	Bomber				
			B-29	B-50	B-17	B-26	Other
ADMINIS-TRATIVE	Hours Flown	23,175	-	-	-	-	-
	Average Aircraft On Hand	73	-	-	-	-	-
	Average Aircraft In Commission	58	-	-	-	-	-
	Av. Hrs. Flown Per A/C On Hand	53	-	-	-	-	-
MINIMUM INDI-VIDUAL TRAINING	Hours Flown	654,049	973	123	6,363	12,335	3,090
	Average Aircraft On Hand	2,452	5	1	33	85	9
	Average Aircraft In Commission	1,604	2	1	25	42	6
	Av. Hrs. Flown Per A/C On Hand	44	32	21	32	24	57
OPERA-TIONAL	Hours Flown	1,215,270	91,445	2,448	3,659	27,109	2,275
	Average Aircraft On Hand	5,285	440	8	16	165	21
	Average Aircraft In Commission	3,293	272	6	10	80	6
	Av. Hrs. Flown Per A/C On Hand	38	35	51	38	27	18
RESEARCH AND DEVELOP-MENT	Hours Flown	33,359	2,815	498	2,696	1,048	1,104
	Average Aircraft On Hand	410	39	6	21	15	14
	Average Aircraft In Commission	197	18	2	14	6	5
	Av. Hrs. Flown Per A/C On Hand	14	12	14	21	12	13
TOTAL FLYING ACTIVE	Hours Flown	1,925,853	95,233	3,069	12,718	40,492	6,469
	Average Aircraft On Hand	8,220	484	15	70	265	44
	Average Aircraft In Commission	5,152	292	9	49	128	17
	Av. Hrs. Flown Per A/C On Hand	39	33	34	30	25	25
b/	All Other Flying Time	16,320	2,213	25	515	628	312
	Grand Total Hours Flown	1,942,173	97,446	3,094	13,233	41,120	6,781

Type of Flying		Fighter					
		F-47	F-51	F-61	F-80	F-82	F-84	Other
ADMINIS-TRATIVE	Hours Flown	-	-	-	-	-	-	-
	Average Aircraft On Hand	-	-	-	-	-	-	-
	Average Aircraft In Commission	-	-	-	-	-	-	-
	Av. Hrs. Flown Per A/C On Hand	-	-	-	-	-	-	-
MINIMUM INDI-VIDUAL TRAINING	Hours Flown	406	5,864	48	1,366	18	1	-
	Average Aircraft On Hand	6	42	1	21	-	-	-
	Average Aircraft In Commission	2	22	-	11	-	-	-
	Av. Hrs. Flown Per A/C On Hand	11	23	8	11	-	-	-
OPERA-TIONAL	Hours Flown	41,351	65,557	9,317	44,391	10,312	11,204	-
	Average Aircraft On Hand	336	616	77	391	103	220	-
	Average Aircraft In Commission	201	374	37	252	40	100	-
	Av. Hrs. Flown Per A/C On Hand	21	18	20	19	17	8	-
RESEARCH AND DEVELOP-MENT	Hours Flown	139	501	429	2,623	970	674	88
	Average Aircraft On Hand	6	9	7	47	18	18	10
	Average Aircraft In Commission	2	5	3	22	6	7	3
	Av. Hrs. Flown Per A/C On Hand	4	9	10	9	9	6	2
TOTAL FLYING ACTIVE	Hours Flown	41,896	71,922	9,794	48,380	11,300	11,879	88
	Average Aircraft On Hand	348	667	85	459	121	238	10
	Average Aircraft In Commission	205	401	40	285	46	107	3
	Av. Hrs. Flown Per A/C On Hand	20	18	19	18	16	8	2
b/	All Other Flying Time	47	988	159	116	179	151	8
	Total Hours Flown	41,943	72,910	9,953	48,496	11,479	12,030	96

847201 O - 49 - 6

TABLE 38.-- UTILIZATION AND MAINTENANCE OF USAF AIRCRAFT, BY TYPE AND MODEL AND BY TYPE OF FLYING: DURING 1948. Continued

July through December 1948

Type of Flying		Reconnaissance						Search And Rescue
		RB-17	RB-29	RB-26	RF-51	RF-80	Other	
ADMINISTRATIVE	Hours Flown Average Aircraft On Hand Average Aircraft In Commission Av. Hrs. Flown Per A/C On Hand	- - - -	- - - -	- - - -	- - - -	- - - -	- - - -	- - - -
MINIMUM INDIVIDUAL TRAINING	Hours Flown Average Aircraft On Hand Average Aircraft In Commission Av. Hrs. Flown Per A/C On Hand	555 4 1 23	543 3 - 30	- - - -	17 - - -	- - - -	1,760 7 5 42	- - - -
OPERATIONAL	Hours Flown Average Aircraft On Hand Average Aircraft In Commission Av. Hrs. Flown Per A/C On Hand	13,098 62 32 35	18,719 85 31 37	6,248 42 25 25	6,046 42 22 24	14,621 84 62 29	6,185 41 27 25	16,729 95 59 29
RESEARCH AND DEVELOPMENT	Hours Flown Average Aircraft On Hand Average Aircraft In Commission Av. Hrs. Flown Per A/C On Hand	- - - -	182 2 - 15	189 3 1 11	122 1 1 20	888 9 6 16	289 4 3 12	9 1 - 2
TOTAL FLYING ACTIVE	Hours Flown Average Aircraft On Hand Average Aircraft In Commission Av. Hrs. Flown Per A/C On Hand	13,653 66 33 34	19,444 90 31 36	6,437 45 26 24	6,185 43 23 24	15,509 93 68 28	8,234 52 35 26	16,738 96 59 29
b/	All Other Flying Time	20	46	451	248	69	111	35
	Total Hours Flown	13,673	19,490	6,888	6,433	15,578	8,345	16,773

Type of Flying		Transport					
		C-45	C-47/117	C-54	C-82	CB-25	Other
ADMINISTRATIVE	Hours Flown Average Aircraft On Hand Average Aircraft In Commission Av. Hrs. Flown Per A/C On Hand	- - - -	17,322 55 45 53	3,087 9 6 57	- - - -	1,154 4 3 48	1,605 5 4 54
MINIMUM INDIVIDUAL TRAINING	Hours Flown Average Aircraft On Hand Average Aircraft In Commission Av. Hrs. Flown Per A/C On Hand	112,364 390 273 48	204,250 581 396 59	6,565 17 10 64	131 3 1 7	21,180 74 46 48	14,191 61 42 39
OPERATIONAL	Hours Flown Average Aircraft On Hand Average Aircraft In Commission Av. Hrs. Flown Per A/C On Hand	2,431 20 11 20	158,643 384 259 69	223,508 256 159 146	27,433 139 74 33	772 3 2 43	22,892 91 42 42
RESEARCH AND DEVELOPMENT	Hours Flown Average Aircraft On Hand Average Aircraft In Commission Av. Hrs. Flown Per A/C On Hand	1,110 11 7 17	3,847 23 14 28	1,878 13 5 24	433 5 2 14	- - - -	1,381 7 4 33
TOTAL FLYING ACTIVE	Hours Flown Average Aircraft On Hand Average Aircraft In Commission Av. Hrs. Flown Per A/C On Hand	115,905 421 291 46	384,062 1,043 714 61	235,038 295 180 133	27,997 147 77 32	23,106 81 51 48	40,069 164 92 41
b/	All Other Flying Time	685	3,366	1,997	1,701	8	195
	Total Hours Flown	116,590	387,428	237,035	29,698	23,114	40,264

TABLE 38.-- UTILIZATION AND MAINTENANCE OF USAF AIRCRAFT, BY TYPE AND MODEL AND BY TYPE OF FLYING: DURING 1948.Continued

July through December 1948

Type of Flying		Trainer					
		T-6	T-7/11	TB-17	TB-25	TB-26	TC-47
ADMINIS-TRATIVE	Hours Flown	-	-	7	-	-	-
	Average Aircraft On Hand	-	-	-	-	-	-
	Average Aircraft In Commission	-	-	-	-	-	-
	Av. Hrs. Flown Per A/C On Hand	-	-	-	-	-	-
MINIMUM INDI-VIDUAL TRAINING	Hours Flown	103,305	15,260	6,988	90,498	15,933	18,475
	Average Aircraft On Hand	498	59	25	304	87*	43
	Average Aircraft In Commission	327	44	17	193	48	31
	Av. Hrs. Flown Per A/C On Hand	35	43	47	50	31	72
OPERA-TIONAL	Hours Flown	231,612	681	3,966	69,032	4,176	7,212
	Average Aircraft On Hand	701	7	17	206	37	22
	Average Aircraft In Commission	567	5	12	134	21	15
	Av. Hrs. Flown Per A/C On Hand	55	15	39	56	19	55
RESEARCH AND DEVELOP-MENT	Hours Flown	499	82	2,099	1,332	782	-
	Average Aircraft On Hand	4	1	15	11	8	-
	Average Aircraft In Commission	3	1	9	7	4	-
	Av. Hrs. Flown Per A/C On Hand	21	14	23	20	16	-
TOTAL FLYING ACTIVE	Hours Flown	335,416	16,023	13,060	160,862	20,891	25,687
	Average Aircraft On Hand	1,203	67	57	521	132	65
	Average Aircraft In Commission	897	50	38	334	73	46
	Av. Hrs. Flown Per A/C On Hand	46	40	38	51	26	66
b/	All Other Flying Time	356	146	25	416	108	2
	Total Hours Flown	335,772	16,169	13,085	161,278	20,999	25,689

Type of Flying		Trainer (Cont'd)			Communications		Gliders and Targets
		TF-51	TF-80	Other	Liaison	Rotary Wing	
ADMINIS-TRATIVE	Hours Flown	-	-	-	-	-	-
	Average Aircraft On Hand	-	-	-	-	-	-
	Average Aircraft In Commission	-	-	-	-	-	-
	Av. Hrs. Flown Per A/C On Hand	-	-	-	-	-	-
MINIMUM INDI-VIDUAL TRAINING	Hours Flown	8,332	-	742	2,122	251	-
	Average Aircraft On Hand	53	-	6	31	3	-
	Average Aircraft In Commission	33	-	3	21	2	-
	Av. Hrs. Flown Per A/C On Hand	26	-	21	11	14	-
OPERA-TIONAL	Hours Flown	23,584	10,159	536	30,606	6,008	1,305
	Average Aircraft On Hand	91	48	6	179	82	152
	Average Aircraft In Commission	62	34	2	140	44	74
	Av. Hrs. Flown Per A/C On Hand	43	35	15	28	12	1
RESEARCH AND DEVELOP-MENT	Hours Flown	619	440	1,345	1,166	670	412
	Average Aircraft On Hand	4	4	16	25	10	23
	Average Aircraft In Commission	3	3	7	10	5	9
	Av. Hrs. Flown Per A/C On Hand	26	18	14	8	11	3
TOTAL FLYING ACTIVE	Hours Flown	32,535	10,599	2,623	33,894	6,929	1,717
	Average Aircraft On Hand	148	52	28	235	95	175
	Average Aircraft In Commission	98	37	12	171	51	83
	Av. Hrs. Flown Per A/C On Hand	37	34	16	24	12	2
b/	All Other Flying Time	36	8	315	373	64	198
	Total Hours Flown	32,571	10,607	2,938	34,267	6,993	1,915

b/ Experimental or "X" models are included in All Other Flying, July through December.

TABLE 39.-- AVIATION FUEL CONSUMPTION

Line No.	Command	Total	Jan	Feb	Mar	Apr	May
1	Total	475,152,982	28,950,823	31,383,940	37,541,603	42,728,392	40,098,838
2	Air Defense Command	15,731,514	905,078	1,231,186	1,448,445	1,682,485	1,556,415
3	Air Materiel Command	32,757,972	2,264,749	2,783,312	3,259,630	3,590,270	3,472,895
4	Air Proving Ground Command	5,173,493	a/	a/	a/	a/	a/
5	Air Training Command	55,733,052	3,171,712	3,384,387	3,999,808	5,192,905	4,742,007
6	Air University	8,259,524	458,252	486,301	621,337	757,516	784,372
7	Chief of Staff	1,615,668	79,479	88,378	132,011	150,211	159,522
8	Continental Air Command	4,493,520	-	-	-	-	-
9	Headquarters Command	10,435,601	623,125	717,961	772,316	871,158	877,904
10	Strategic Air Command	99,347,047	8,032,495	7,736,965	8,358,426	9,205,345	7,984,912
11	Tactical Air Command	41,794,274	2,673,824	2,740,717	3,860,765	4,873,643	4,847,822
12	Military Air Transport Service (world-wide)	64,557,530	4,104,616	5,447,047	5,861,026	6,845,680	7,020,145
13	Alaskan Air Command	9,192,280	539,966	605,440	816,147	933,506	1,026,689
14	Caribbean Air Command	12,303,642	816,568	932,385	1,208,353	1,345,953	1,478,463
15	US Air Forces in Europe	13,537,564	1,000,814	943,930	1,490,434	1,559,641	1,342,330
16	Far East Air Forces	54,614,055	3,788,640	3,716,886	5,124,927	5,124,019	4,214,427
17	Pacific Air Command	5,328,975	363,059	469,062	463,172	482,336	505,011
18	Other Overseas b/	6,736,289	103,446	99,983	124,806	113,724	85,924
19	Operation Vittles	33,540,982	-	-	-	-	-

a/ Included with Air Materiel Command.
b/ Includes Army Advisory Group (China) and JhUSMC; and during October through December, Strategic Air Command, Tactical Air Command, and Chief of Staff overseas units.

OF USAF AIRCRAFT DURING 1948, BY COMMAND

Jun	Jul	Aug	Sep	Oct	Nov	Dec	Line No.
39,613,090	43,095,103	46,310,466	45,726,309	42,627,106	38,847,807	38,227,505	1
1,674,532	1,708,202	1,699,003	1,428,931	1,293,192	1,104,045	-	2
2,556,177	2,634,419	2,856,209	2,515,023	2,636,350	2,088,975	2,049,963	3
796,978	794,543	725,115	815,150	792,447	624,080	625,180	4
4,744,359	5,023,234	5,740,502	5,478,765	4,734,088	5,314,266	4,207,019	5
746,258	683,388	740,503	807,148	862,042	680,317	632,090	6
151,602	144,297	166,468	159,487	139,789	120,911	123,513	7
-	-	-	-	-	-	4,493,520	8
915,349	874,108	985,917	955,965	1,000,354	932,360	909,084	9
9,551,196	9,472,831	10,063,118	9,301,582	6,817,794	6,190,012	6,632,371	10
3,933,374	3,976,957	4,368,912	4,205,950	3,505,240	2,807,070	-	11
6,170,935	6,428,141	4,886,889	5,007,660	4,597,837	4,006,725	4,180,829	12
1,071,810	770,909	937,787	775,521	633,329	540,067	541,109	13
1,430,251	748,803	832,768	937,629	920,562	806,000	845,907	14
1,259,107	614,915	965,857	1,297,515	1,144,758	1,163,522	754,741	15
3,978,851	4,481,328	4,880,749	5,059,020	4,834,832	4,838,749	4,571,627	16
541,113	419,144	526,234	426,029	430,412	344,339	334,064	17
91,198	123,549	109,166	92,711	1,638,736	2,611,289	1,541,757	18
-	4,146,335	5,825,269	6,464,223	6,645,344	4,675,080	5,784,731	19

TABLE 40.-- AVIATION FUEL CONSUMPTION OF USAF AIRCRAFT, BY TYPE AND MODEL-DURING 1948

Type and Model	Total Jan-Jun	Jan	Feb	Mar	Apr	May	Jun
Total	220,316,686	28,950,823	31,383,940	37,541,603	42,728,392	40,098,838	39,613,090
Bomber - Total	89,535,295	13,078,532	13,464,091	14,802,631	17,260,125	15,003,940	15,926,076
B-29	46,130,039	7,143,976	7,542,102	7,482,988	8,810,106	6,759,886	8,390,981
B-17	11,094,288	1,839,296	1,747,287	1,850,906	1,820,159	2,038,453	1,798,187
B-25	20,806,029	2,641,711	2,725,651	3,498,249	4,272,436	3,807,133	3,860,799
A-26	10,976,553	1,412,185	1,399,905	1,918,092	2,236,300	2,284,623	1,725,448
Other	528,486	41,364	49,146	52,396	121,124	113,795	150,661
Fighter - Total	35,377,158	3,603,082	4,683,761	6,486,370	7,397,405	6,748,347	6,458,193
F-47	5,731,367	751,946	721,319	1,227,539	1,191,731	942,247	896,585
F-51	8,070,842	1,101,139	1,206,975	1,396,045	1,459,340	1,632,660	1,274,683
F-61	2,288,953	239,747	344,770	471,288	473,986	393,258	365,904
F-80	17,060,626	1,401,770	2,122,059	3,052,472	3,789,821	3,364,525	3,329,979
F-84	1,959,189	70,844	242,841	304,054	434,522	369,175	537,753
Other	266,181	37,636	45,797	34,972	48,005	46,482	53,289
Reconnaissance - Total	12,771,554	1,700,483	1,609,805	2,241,918	2,394,535	2,619,520	2,105,293
F-2	174,101	16,930	25,898	34,445	28,977	28,404	39,447
F-6	654,702	69,456	66,288	112,741	126,348	153,712	126,157
F-9	1,823,118	137,128	110,529	161,781	465,409	577,267	371,004
F-13	2,847,945	310,516	272,856	494,963	545,175	653,090	571,345
FB-17	855,545	240,383	226,601	388,561	-	-	-
FA-26	1,404,059	208,459	209,310	274,416	295,612	255,233	160,529
FP-80	4,627,788	670,035	654,718	824,964	863,083	867,223	747,765
Other	384,296	47,576	43,105	50,047	69,931	84,591	89,046
Search and Rescue	278,116	34,973	34,529	29,138	40,876	80,025	58,575
Transport - Total	74,667,551	9,523,553	10,554,595	12,682,172	14,163,230	14,202,862	13,541,139
C-45	4,483,036	632,154	623,607	738,016	847,208	798,064	843,987
C-46	2,880,202	474,457	496,273	531,984	434,913	433,827	508,748
C-47/117	33,197,141	4,364,078	4,466,206	5,700,276	6,194,402	6,193,525	6,278,654
C-54	28,006,924	3,407,055	4,203,942	4,751,763	5,382,572	5,482,253	4,779,339
C-82	4,652,166	554,406	656,501	709,339	993,683	950,214	788,023
Other	1,448,082	91,403	108,066	250,794	310,452	344,979	342,388
Trainer - Total	7,250,111	947,816	978,206	1,129,585	1,389,020	1,364,611	1,440,873
AT-6	6,698,909	886,056	898,750	1,052,698	1,299,539	1,248,258	1,313,608
AT-7/AT-11	543,182	60,372	74,987	76,149	89,219	115,965	126,490
Other	8,020	1,388	4,469	738	262	388	775
Communication - Total	430,906	61,557	57,592	68,540	82,388	78,879	81,950
Liaison	319,577	47,941	41,876	48,376	63,883	56,648	60,853
Rotary wing	111,329	13,616	15,716	20,164	18,505	22,231	21,097
Gliders and Targets	5,895	827	1,361	1,249	813	654	991

TABLE 40.-- AVIATION FUEL CONSUMPTION OF USAF AIRCRAFT, BY TYPE AND MODEL-DURING Continued

Type and Model	Total Jul-Dec	Jul	Aug	Sep	Oct	Nov	Dec
Total	254,836,296	43,095,103	46,310,466	45,728,309	42,627,106	38,847,807	38,227,505
Bomber - Total	53,204,017	9,239,800	9,414,751	9,407,953	8,557,344	8,331,436	8,252,733
B-36	854,549	47,143	128,382	230,049	38,079	119,582	291,314
B-29	40,977,019	7,577,010	7,516,183	7,039,663	6,386,822	6,440,162	6,017,179
B-17	2,731,795	540,729	482,776	514,445	496,997	325,121	371,727
B-26	5,814,104	817,621	819,073	1,084,737	1,185,126	969,918	937,629
Other	2,826,550	257,297	468,337	539,059	450,320	476,653	634,884
Fighter - Total	33,061,954	5,828,616	6,656,881	6,162,229	5,101,350	4,863,356	4,449,522
F-47	4,325,450	823,693	873,904	790,747	711,058	585,081	540,967
F-51	4,613,661	863,481	791,871	778,825	755,553	722,324	701,607
F-61	1,583,638	332,192	357,278	323,503	266,989	166,113	137,563
F-80	17,225,077	2,815,016	3,394,520	3,338,476	2,716,476	2,666,869	2,293,720
F-84	3,881,018	883,937	1,050,657	797,701	330,840	375,459	442,424
Other	1,433,110	110,297	188,651	132,977	320,434	347,510	333,241
Reconnaissance - Total	17,473,484	2,663,778	3,058,184	3,159,007	3,010,017	2,692,090	2,890,408
RB-17	2,848,677	348,530	413,507	529,662	513,886	476,368	561,724
RB-29	7,376,951	1,131,246	1,263,108	1,378,628	1,239,120	1,017,805	1,247,044
RB-26	1,021,205	172,553	229,811	208,136	158,663	135,728	116,314
RF-51	410,059	84,904	67,813	72,810	69,321	54,855	60,356
RF-61	496,824	55,876	94,901	81,026	77,639	108,228	79,154
RF-80	4,978,715	819,474	912,602	827,360	790,407	848,943	779,929
RC-45	235,450	36,707	58,339	34,802	44,162	34,350	27,090
Other	105,603	14,488	13,103	26,583	16,819	15,813	18,797
Search and Rescue	2,734,719	337,713	448,556	491,564	479,248	549,006	428,627
Transport - Total	103,066,218	17,409,423	18,120,208	18,497,323	18,096,264	14,971,702	15,971,297
C-45	4,756,631	830,772	876,937	851,479	818,755	694,732	683,956
C-46	3,224,805	505,234	522,005	450,747	579,334	572,127	595,358
C-47/C-117	35,964,024	7,224,429	6,838,589	6,562,386	5,528,289	4,770,640	5,039,691
C-54	46,270,603	6,835,332	7,739,751	8,218,403	8,915,895	6,959,794	7,601,428
C-82	5,293,886	866,800	924,490	1,088,043	918,225	787,402	618,926
CB-17	1,979,908	306,178	282,375	358,522	362,752	300,615	369,466
CB-25	3,186,305	509,629	528,581	544,330	579,813	531,102	492,850
CB-26	565,489	65,451	88,106	110,965	110,129	102,281	88,557
Other	1,914,567	265,598	319,374	312,448	283,072	253,010	481,065
Trainer - Total	44,784,490	7,527,481	8,513,965	7,928,525	7,297,825	7,353,828	6,162,866
T-6	8,502,217	1,402,784	1,606,808	1,533,345	1,315,702	1,470,301	1,173,277
T-7/11	641,586	130,479	106,829	110,233	117,407	104,516	72,122
TB-17	2,733,568	453,589	530,475	457,359	494,933	435,989	361,223
TB-25	20,621,475	3,714,294	4,200,292	3,526,177	3,270,306	3,226,543	2,683,863
TE-26	3,376,797	411,076	568,804	620,585	697,820	499,153	579,359
TF-80	3,343,791	510,065	453,491	698,337	500,098	610,181	571,619
Other	5,565,056	905,194	1,047,266	982,489	901,559	1,007,145	721,403
Communications - Total	471,823	80,997	88,146	77,092	81,258	80,758	63,272
Liaison	324,335	65,706	61,615	48,335	51,321	54,602	41,756
Rotary Wing	147,488	14,291	26,531	28,757	30,237	26,156	21,516
Targets	39,591	7,290	9,775	4,616	3,500	5,630	8,780

TABLE 41 -- NUMBER AND RATE OF USAF AIRCRAFT ACCIDENTS, BY TYPE AND MODEL OF AIRCRAFT: QUARTERLY-1948

(Rates are expressed in accidents per 100,000 flying hours)

Type and Model	Flying Hours	Major Accidents No.	Rate	Fatal Accidents No.	Rate	Fatalities a/ No.	Rate	Aircraft Wrecked b/ No.	Rate	Minor Accidents No.	Rate	All Accidents No.	Rate
Total	4,158,794	1,586	38	210	5	574	14	538	13	783	19	2,369	57
First Quarter - Total													
USAF (Excl. Air National Guard)	850,514	367	43	39	5	100	12	108	13	181	21	548	64
Bomber - Total	194,530	52	27	5	3	31	16	10	5	16	8	68	35
B-17	32,179	8	25	1	3	9	28	1	3	2	6	10	31
B-25	66,120	11	17	2	3	8	12	3	5	2	3	13	20
B-26	37,427	18	48	0	0	0	0	2	5	2	5	20	53
B-29	58,484	15	26	2	3	14	24	4	7	10	17	25	43
B-49	-	0	0	0	0	0	0	0	0	0	0	0	0
B-50	254	0	0	0	0	0	0	0	0	0	0	0	0
Other	70	0	0	0	0	0	0	0	0	0	0	0	0
Transport - Total	295,342	50	17	7	2	27	10	13	4	40	14	90	30
C-45	52,478	20	38	2	4	4	8	5	10	11	21	31	59
C-46, (C-113)	10,182	1	10	0	0	0	0	1	10	2	20	3	29
C-47/53, (C-117)	156,223	15	10	3	2	25	16	5	3	22	14	37	24
C-54	64,013	6	9	0	0	0	0	0	0	4	6	10	16
C-64	411	1	243	0	0	0	0	1	243	1	243	2	487
C-74	505	1	198	0	0	0	0	0	0	0	0	1	198
C-82	10,859	6	55	0	0	0	0	1	9	0	0	6	55
C-97	662	0	0	0	0	0	0	0	0	0	0	0	0
Other	9	0	0	0	0	0	0	0	0	0	0	0	0
Fighter - Total	126,213	159	115	17	13	21	17	61	48	28	22	178	141
F-47	26,829	38	142	5	19	5	19	14	52	4	15	42	157
F-51	61,514	62	101	5	8	5	8	29	47	11	18	73	119
F-61	7,787	9	116	2	26	4	51	3	39	6	77	15	193
F-80	27,132	32	118	5	18	7	26	12	44	7	26	39	144
F-82	834	2	240	0	0	0	0	0	0	0	0	2	240
F-84	2,088	7	335	0	0	0	0	3	144	0	0	7	335
Other	28	0	0	0	0	0	0	0	0	0	0	0	0
Trainer - Total	215,640	91	42	10	5	16	7	19	9	80	37	171	79
Liaison - Total	14,373	12	83	1	7	2	14	3	21	16	111	28	195
Rotary Wing - Total . .	2,384	2	84	0	0	0	0	0	0	1	42	3	126
Miscellaneous c/													
All Other Types . . .	2,030	10	-	1	-	1	-	2	-	0	-	10	-
Second Quarter - Total													
USAF (Excl. Air National Guard)	1,114,319	386	35	49	4	132	12	131	12	199	18	585	52
Bomber - Total	239,875	46	19	8	3	44	18	13	5	16	7	62	26
B-17	34,024	5	15	1	3	5	15	2	6	5	15	10	29
B-25	92,650	12	13	1	1	4	4	3	3	2	2	14	15
B-26	47,717	21	44	2	4	5	10	4	8	2	4	23	48
B-29	64,788	7	11	3	5	25	39	3	5	7	11	14	22
B-49	-	1	-	1	-	5	-	1	-	0	-	1	-
B-50	627	0	0	0	0	0	0	0	0	0	0	0	0
Other	69	0	0	0	0	0	0	0	0	0	0	0	0
Transport - Total . . .	374,543	35	9	5	1	20	5	11	3	33	9	68	18
C-45	64,356	16	25	2	3	9	14	5	8	8	12	24	37
C-46, (C-113)	9,366	1	11	0	0	0	0	0	0	0	0	1	11
C-47/53, (C-117)	202,235	10	5	2	1	8	4	4	2	16	8	26	13
C-54	79,515	4	5	1	1	3	4	2	3	6	8	10	13
C-74	1,336	0	0	0	0	0	0	0	0	0	0	0	0
C-82	16,452	3	18	0	0	0	0	0	0	2	12	5	30
C-97	930	1	108	0	0	0	0	0	0	1	108	2	215
Other	353	0	0	0	0	0	0	0	0	0	0	0	0
Fighter - Total	156,348	162	104	24	15	29	19	69	44	38	24	200	128
F-47	29,462	33	112	3	10	4	14	18	61	1	3	34	115
F-51	73,679	69	94	13	18	12	16	26	35	18	24	87	118
F-61	8,904	7	79	2	22	4	45	6	67	3	34	10	112
F-80	38,808	38	98	4	10	7	18	14	36	16	41	54	139
F-82	1,023	3	293	0	0	0	0	1	98	0	0	3	293
F-84	4,428	12	271	2	45	2	45	4	90	0	0	12	271
Other	42	0	0	0	0	0	0	0	0	0	0	0	0
Trainer - Total	315,816	119	38	12	4	19	6	29	9	107	34	226	72
Liaison - Total	21,019	15	71	0	0	0	0	5	24	3	14	18	86
Rotary Wing - Total . .	3,046	6	197	0	0	0	0	2	66	2	66	8	263
Miscellaneous d/													
All Other Types . . .	3,672	3	-	0	-	0	-	2	-	0	-	3	-

a/ Fatalities include all personnel killed and/or missing as a result of USAF aircraft Accidents
b/ Aircraft wrecked include missing aircraft   c/ Includes A-10, Q-14, G-15, Vampire   d/ Includes A-10, Q-14, DC-3
e/ Rate not significant   f/ Includes A-10, A-12, Q-14, German Jet Helicopter   g/ Includes A-10, Q-14, XR-12

TABLE 41 -- NUMBER AND RATE OF USAF AIRCRAFT ACCIDENTS, BY TYPE AND MODEL OF AIRCRAFT QUARTERLY 1948
Continued

(Rates are expressed in accidents per 100,000 flying hours)

Type and Model	Flying Hours	Major Accidents No.	Major Accidents Rate	Fatal Accidents No.	Fatal Accidents Rate	Fatalities a/ No.	Fatalities a/ Rate	Aircraft Wrecked b/ No.	Aircraft Wrecked b/ Rate	Minor Accidents No.	Minor Accidents Rate	All Accidents No.	All Accidents Rate
Third Quarter - Total USAF (Excl Air National Guard)	1,188,046	442	37	69	6	185	16	150	13	212	18	654	55
Bomber - Total	236,081	59	25	17	7	103	43	21	9	25	11	84	36
B-17	30,948	7	23	1	3	5	16	3	10	4	13	11	36
B-25	103,946	12	12	2	2	1	1	5	5	6	6	18	17
B-26	35,566	16	45	3	8	8	22	4	11	5	14	21	59
B-29	63,661	21	33	10	16	86	135	8	13	8	13	29	46
B-36	591	0	0	0	0	0	0	0	0	1	169	1	169
B-45	444	2	450	1	225	2	450	1	225	1	225	3	676
B-46	2	1	a/	0	0	0	0	0	0	0	0	1	a/
B-50	878	0	0	0	0	0	0	0	0	0	0	0	0
Others	45	0	0	0	0	0	0	0	0	0	0	0	0
Transports - Total	444,580	58	13	5	1	23	5	13	3	27	6	85	19
C-45	64,838	10	15	0	0	0	0	0	0	3	5	13	20
C-46, (C-113)	10,343	5	48	0	0	0	0	0	0	0	0	5	48
C-47/53, (C-117)	235,590	29	12	5	2	23	10	10	4	13	6	42	18
C-54	113,878	9	8	0	0	0	0	2	2	10	9	19	17
C-64	495	1	202	0	0	0	0	0	0	0	0	1	202
C-74	1,137	0	0	0	0	0	0	0	0	0	0	0	0
C-82	17,063	4	23	0	0	0	0	1	6	1	6	5	29
C-97	1,079	0	0	0	0	0	0	0	0	0	0	0	0
Other	157	0	0	0	0	0	0	0	0	0	0	0	0
Fighter - Total	142,181	187	132	31	22	32	23	90	63	39	27	226	159
F-47	24,535	46	187	9	37	9	37	24	98	7	29	53	216
F-51	58,754	62	106	8	14	8	14	28	48	14	24	76	129
F-61	7,583	6	79	1	13	1	13	3	40	0	0	6	79
F-80	39,197	44	112	10	26	10	26	23	59	14	36	58	148
F-82	3,667	5	136	1	27	2	55	2	55	3	82	8	218
F-84	8,405	24	286	2	24	2	24	10	119	1	12	25	297
Other	40	0	0	0	0	0	0	0	0	0	0	0	0
Trainer - Total	340,125	108	32	15	4	27	8	16	5	111	33	219	64
Liaison - Total	18,660	17	91	1	5	1	5	4	21	6	32	23	123
Rotary Wing - Total	3,407	6	176	0	0	0	0	3	88	1	29	7	205
Miscellaneous f/ All Other Types	3,012	7	-	0	-	0	-	3	-	3	-	10	-
Fourth Quarter - Total USAF (Excl Air National Guard)	1,005,918	291	39	53	5	177	18	149	15	191	19	582	58
Bomber - Total	214,514	52	24	8	4	87	41	22	10	26	12	78	36
B-17	30,306	10	33	1	3	5	16	5	16	1	3	11	36
B-25	85,622	12	14	2	2	13	15	4	5	3	4	15	18
B-26	39,455	8	20	0	0	0	0	3	8	6	15	14	35
B-29	55,984	20	36	4	7	53	95	8	14	16	29	36	64
B-36	664	0	0	0	0	0	0	0	0	0	0	0	0
B-45	232	1	431	0	0	0	0	0	0	0	0	1	431
B-50	2,216	1	45	1	45	16	722	2	90	0	0	1	45
Other	35	0	0	0	0	0	0	0	0	0	0	0	0
Transport - Total	384,138	68	18	17	4	57	15	30	8	44	11	112	29
C-45	56,574	16	28	3	5	5	9	6	11	6	11	22	39
C-46, (C-113)	11,677	2	17	0	0	0	0	1	9	2	17	4	34
C-47/53, (C-117)	177,507	18	10	7	4	32	18	11	6	18	10	36	20
C-54	123,255	22	18	5	4	12	10	8	6	16	13	38	31
C-64	110	0	0	0	0	0	0	0	0	2	a/	2	a/
C-74	1,878	0	0	0	0	0	0	0	0	0	0	0	0
C-82	12,635	9	71	2	16	8	63	4	32	0	0	9	71
C-122	-	1	-	0	0	0	0	0	0	0	0	1	-
Other	502	0	0	0	0	0	0	0	0	0	0	0	0
Fighter - Total	121,577	157	129	19	16	19	16	67	55	36	30	193	159
F-47	17,474	18	103	3	17	3	17	6	34	6	34	24	137
F-51	51,860	57	110	8	15	8	15	26	50	12	23	69	133
F-61	5,189	5	96	0	0	0	0	1	19	3	58	8	154
F-80	35,569	40	112	8	22	8	22	23	65	10	28	50	141
F-82	7,812	21	269	0	0	0	0	3	38	5	64	26	333
F-84	3,625	15	414	0	0	0	0	8	221	0	0	15	414
F-86	41	1	a/	0	0	0	0	0	0	0	0	1	a/
Other	7	0	0	0	0	0	0	0	0	0	0	0	0
Trainer - Total	262,602	89	34	6	2	9	3	20	8	78	30	167	64
Liaison - Total	16,256	12	74	1	6	2	12	5	31	3	18	15	92
Rotary Wing - Total	3,698	8	216	1	27	1	27	4	108	2	54	10	270
Miscellaneous g/ All Other Types	3,133	5	160	1	32	2	64	1	32	2	64	7	223

Source: The Inspector General, USAF-Office of the Air Inspector - Flying Safety Division

PART IV
USAF RESERVE FORCES..................

USAF RESERVE FORCES

The tables in this section are designed to reflect over-all current statistical facts relative to USAF Reserve Forces aircraft, aircraft flying time, aircraft utilization and related data.

The Air Reserve tables present a tabulation of airplanes on hand, By Air Force Area, and by type and model of airplane; a summary of Air Reserve monthly activities, which includes flying time and fuel consumption of aircraft and the average number of pilots and the accident rates for 100,000 flying hours. Flying Time of Air Force Pilots on Inactive Duty status during 1948 is also known.

A tabulation of airplanes on hand in the Air National Guard by Air Force Area and State or Territory and also by type and model of airplane are presented in Tables 45 and 46. A summary of Air National Guard monthly activities is presented in Table 47.

TABLE 42.--AIRPLANES ON HAND IN THE AIR RESERVE, BY AIR FORCE AREA AND TYPE AND MODEL OF AIRPLANE--MONTHLY-1948

Note:--The data below are included in other continental US airplane inventory tables reflected elsewhere in this volume. (Figures are as of end of month)

Air Force Area and Type and Model	Jan	Feb	Mar	Apr	May	Jun
Total	1,244	1,233	1,229	1,238	1,209	1,213
1st Air Force - Total	240	240	237	240	221	213
Bomber - Total	-	-	-	-	1	5
A-26	-	-	-	-	-	4
TA-26	-	-	-	-	1	1
Trainer - Total	240	240	237	240	220	208
AT-6	184	185	185	184	165	156
AT-7	3	3	3	3	3	3
AT-11	53	52	49	53	52	49
2nd Air Force - Total	291	287	288	288	285	284
Trainer - Total	291	287	288	288	285	284
AT-6	220	218	219	218	217	216
AT-7	2	2	2	2	1	1
AT-11	69	67	67	68	67	67
4th Air Force - Total	160	161	160	159	159	161
Trainer - Total	160	161	160	159	159	161
AT-6	116	116	114	115	116	118
AT-7	6	6	6	6	6	6
AT-11	38	39	40	38	37	37
10th Air Force - Total	151	148	144	143	142	145
Bomber - Total	-	-	-	-	-	4
A-26	-	-	-	-	-	4
Trainer - Total	151	148	144	143	142	141
AT-6	109	107	104	104	104	104
AT-7	4	4	3	3	3	3
AT-11	38	37	37	36	35	34
11th Air Force - Total	256	255	256	258	254	258
Trainer - Total	256	255	256	258	254	258
AT-6	196	196	198	198	194	197
AT-7	1	1	1	1	1	1
AT-11	59	58	57	59	59	60
14th Air Force - Total	146	142	144	150	148	152
Trainer - Total	146	142	144	150	148	152
AT-6	112	109	114	113	111	114
AT-11	34	33	30	37	37	38

TABLE 42.— AIRPLANES ON HAND IN THE AIR RESERVE, BY AIR FORCE AREA, AND TYPE AND MODEL OF AIRPLANE—MONTHLY-1948-Continued

Note:—The data below are excluded from other continental US airplane inventory tables reflected elsewhere in this volume. Figures are as of end of month.

Air Force Area and Type and Model	Jul	Aug	Sep	Oct	Nov	Dec
Total	1,210	1,210	1,221	1,200	1,213	1,250
1st. Air Force - Total	417	424	467	453	455	474
Bomber - Total	4	4	6	6	6	11
B-26	4	4	6	6	6	11
Trainer - Total	413	420	461	447	449	462
T-6	313	321	353	340	341	351
T-7	4	4	4	4	4	4
T-11	95	94	103	102	103	106
TB-26	1	1	1	1	1	1
Transport - Total	-	-	-	-	-	1
C-46	-	-	-	-	-	1
4th. Air Force - Total	163	160	163	164	167	184
Bomber - Total	-	-	-	-	3	12
B-26	-	-	-	-	3	12
Trainer - Total	163	160	163	164	164	170
T-6	119	119	120	119	120	122
T-7	6	6	6	6	6	6
T-11	38	35	37	39	38	41
TB-26	-	-	-	-	-	1
Transport - Total	-	-	-	-	-	2
C-46	-	-	-	-	-	2
10th. Air Force - Total	340	339	299	288	291	290
Bomber - Total	-	-	-	-	4	6
B-26	-	-	-	-	4	6
Trainer - Total	340	339	298	287	286	283
T-6	259	260	226	217	215	211
T-7	1	1	1	1	1	2
T-11	80	78	71	69	70	70
Transport - Total	-	-	1	1	1	1
C-45	-	-	1	1	1	-
C-46	-	-	-	-	-	1
14th. Air Force - Total	290	287	292	295	300	302
Bomber - Total	4	4	4	7	12	13
B-26	4	4	4	7	12	13
Trainer - Total	286	283	288	288	288	287
T-6	216	213	218	218	217	217
T-7	3	3	2	2	2	2
T-11	67	67	68	68	69	68
Transport - Total	-	-	-	-	-	2
C-46	-	-	-	-	-	2

TABLE 43.-- SUMMARY OF AIR FORCE RESERVE ACTIVITIES-DURING 1948

Month	Flying Active Aircraft				Average Number of Pilots	Accident Rate Per 100,000 Hours	Fuel Con-sumption	Total Hours Flown
	Hours Flown	Average Aircraft On Hand	Percent of A/C in Commission	Average Hours Flown Per A/C On Hand				
Jan	29,669	1,212	77	24	9,719	27	851,559	29,672
Feb	30,462	1,178	76	26	13,111	49	927,521	30,462
Mar	38,761	1,175	78	33	15,279	32	1,171,058	38,793
Apr	48,010	1,183	79	41	16,382	23	1,478,690	48,034
May	51,777	1,174	79	44	15,900	45	1,596,393	51,848
Jun	60,531	1,175	78	52	15,824	27	1,841,476	60,543
Jul	56,888	1,148	79	50	14,710	18	1,735,301	56,970
Aug	52,730	1,151	77	46	17,172	26	1,598,870	52,867
Sep	45,369	1,163	78	39	16,541	24	1,397,142	45,486
Oct	38,180	1,166	80	33	18,547	29	1,202,304	38,202
Nov	31,615	1,170	81	27	17,401	27	1,064,628	31,686
Dec	28,071	1,210	82	23	15,236	32	1,010,741	28,073

TABLE 44.-- FLYING TIME OF AIR FORCE PILOTS ON INACTIVE DUTY STATUS DURING 1948

Month	1st. Pilot Hours Flown On Reserve A/C	1st. Pilot Hours Flown On USAF A/C	Total 1st. Pilot Hours Flown	Number Reserve Pilots Receiving Training a/	Average Hours Flown Per Pilot
Jan	24,383	1,392	25,775	9,719	2.7
Feb	25,458	1,072	26,530	13,111	2.0
Mar	31,898	2,144	34,042	15,279	2.2
Apr	40,531	2,294	42,825	16,332	2.6
May	44,745	2,291	47,036	15,900	3.0
Jun	52,828	3,721	56,549	15,824	3.6
Jul	47,069	2,583	49,652	14,710	3.4
Aug	43,595	2,625	46,220	17,171	2.7
Sep	35,907	1,865	37,772	16,541	2.3
Oct	29,541	1,252	30,793	18,547	1.7
Nov	24,723	934	25,657	17,401	1.5
Dec	20,813	801	21,614	15,236	1.4

a/ Includes pilots receiving either flying training or ground training or both.

TABLE 45 -- AIRPLANES ON HAND IN AIR NATIONAL GUARD, BY AIR FORCE AREA AND STATE OR TERRITORY: MONTHLY-1948

(Figures are as of end of month)

Air Force Area and Location	Jan	Feb	Mar	Apr	May	Jun
Total	1,930	1,966	1,998	2,028	2,043	2,034
Continental US - Total	1,904	1,938	1,972	2,000	2,004	1,991
1st Air Force - Total	305	321	341	338	339	334
Connecticut	28	30	31	34	35	34
Delaware	32	32	32	32	34	32
Maine	19	20	20	19	19	19
Massachusetts	70	71	63	59	60	61
New Hampshire	39	39	39	39	39	38
New Jersey	41	42	42	40	40	40
New York	35	47	74	74	74	72
Rhode Island	1	1	1	1	-	-
Vermont	40	39	39	40	38	38
2nd Air Force - Total	504	507	509	509	496	482
Colorado	39	38	38	38	39	39
Illinois	56	59	62	61	61	59
Iowa	71	71	71	71	70	60
Kansas	33	33	32	32	32	32
Michigan	38	39	40	39	38	43
Minnesota	33	32	32	33	33	33
Missouri	64	64	64	64	64	63
Nebraska	34	34	34	34	27	28
North Dakota	40	39	39	39	33	34
South Dakota	35	36	35	36	37	36
Wisconsin	26	27	27	27	27	27
Wyoming	35	35	35	35	35	28
4th Air Force - Total	312	311	311	309	317	303
Arizona	34	34	35	34	35	36
California	102	102	101	101	106	94
Idaho	38	38	38	37	37	37
Montana	25	25	25	25	26	26
Nevada	-	-	-	-	-	4
Oregon	41	40	40	40	42	41
Utah	36	36	36	36	36	30
Washington	36	36	36	36	36	35
10th Air Force - Total	186	199	197	196	197	197
Arkansas	37	33	33	33	33	32
Louisiana	22	22	21	21	22	21
New Mexico	15	22	22	22	22	27
Oklahoma	60	60	60	60	60	53
Texas	52	62	61	60	60	64
11th Air Force - Total	320	311	310	310	317	340
District of Col	42	42	42	42	42	41
Indiana	31	32	36	36	38	44
Kentucky	32	27	27	27	27	27
Maryland	39	38	37	38	37	37
Ohio	70	72	72	73	73	85
Pennsylvania	44	44	44	44	44	44
Virginia	35	34	34	36	36	36
West Virginia	27	22	18	14	20	26
14th Air Force - Total	277	289	304	338	338	335
Alabama	31	37	37	35	41	42
Florida	38	38	38	38	39	34
Georgia	75	73	81	111	107	107
Mississippi	31	32	33	34	32	33
North Carolina	1	11	16	21	20	20
South Carolina	29	27	27	27	27	27
Tennessee	72	71	72	72	72	72
Overseas - Total	26	28	26	28	39	43
Pacific Air Comd Hawaii	24	26	24	24	23	23
Carribbean Area Puerto Rico	2	2	2	4	16	20

TABLE 45 -- AIRPLANES ON HAND IN AIR NATIONAL GUARD, BY AIR FORCE AREA AND STATE OR TERRITORY: MONTHLY-1948
Continued

(Figures are as of end of month)

Air Force Area and Location	Jul	Aug	Sep	Oct	Nov
Total	2,048	2,045	2,029	2,047	2,069
Continental US - Total	1,998	1,988	1,975	1,991	2,013
1st Air Force - Total	690	702	698	697	702
Connecticut	34	29	29	29	29
Delaware	32	32	31	31	31
District of Columbia	42	42	41	41	41
Kentucky	26	26	26	26	25
Maine	19	26	28	27	29
Maryland	37	37	37	37	37
Massachusetts	61	59	59	61	62
Michigan	61	62	62	61	61
New Jersey	40	40	40	40	40
New Hampshire	37	37	37	37	37
New York	72	85	85	86	87
Ohio	85	86	84	84	84
Pennsylvania	44	43	43	43	43
Rhode Island	-	-	-	-	1
Vermont	38	38	37	35	35
Virginia	37	34	34	34	34
West Virginia	25	26	25	25	25
4th Air Force - Total	289	287	285	284	289
Arizona	28	28	28	27	28
California	95	94	93	93	97
Idaho	32	28	27	27	27
Montana	25	28	28	28	28
Nevada	17	17	17	17	17
Oregon	35	34	34	34	34
Utah	29	30	30	30	30
Washington	28	28	28	28	28
10th Air Force - Total	486	483	475	472	470
Colorado	34	34	33	33	31
Illinois	65	64	59	59	59
Indiana	50	50	49	49	49
Iowa	54	55	54	52	49
Kansas	32	31	31	31	31
Minnesota	34	32	32	32	32
Missouri	62	61	61	61	61
Nebraska	35	38	37	37	41
North Dakota	33	32	32	32	32
South Dakota	30	29	30	30	29
Wisconsin	29	29	29	29	29
Wyoming	28	28	28	27	27
14th Air Force - Total	533	516	517	538	552
Alabama	44	44	45	46	45
Arkansas	25	25	25	25	27
Florida	31	30	30	35	37
Georgia	111	101	102	108	112
Louisiana	19	19	19	19	20
Mississippi	35	33	33	32	33
New Mexico	29	29	29	29	34
North Carolina	22	23	24	24	24
Oklahoma	53	52	52	52	51
South Carolina	26	26	26	26	26
Tennessee	65	63	62	63	63
Texas	73	71	70	79	80
Overseas - Total	50	57	54	56	56
Pacific Air Command					
Hawaii	28	28	27	27	27
Caribbean Area					
Puerto Rico	22	29	27	29	29

TABLE 45. -- AIRPLANES ON HAND IN AIR NATIONAL GUARD, BY AIR FORCE AREA AND STATE OR TERRITORY: MONTHLY-1948
Continued

(Figures are as of end of month)

Air Force Area and Location	Dec
Total	2,148
Continental US - Total	2,090
1st. Air Force - Total	326
Connecticut	28
Maine	34
Massachusetts	61
New Jersey	40
New Hampshire	37
New York	90
Rhode Island	4
Vermont	32
4th. Air Force - Total	299
Arizona	28
California	106
Idaho	24
Montana	32
Nevada	17
Oregon	34
Utah	30
Washington	28
9th. Air Force - Total	342
District of Columbia	41
Delaware	31
Kentucky	29
Maryland	37
Ohio	105
Pennsylvania	41
Virginia	33
West Virginia	25
10th. Air Force - Total	568
Colorado	31
Illinois	71
Indiana	57
Iowa	49
Kansas	29
Michigan	69
Minnesota	32
Missouri	60
North Dakota	32
Nebraska	46
South Dakota	26
Wisconsin	39
Wyoming	27
12th. Air Force - Total	343
Alabama	45
Florida	38
Georgia	111
Mississippi	32
North Carolina	29
South Carolina	26
Tennessee	62
14th. Air Force - Total	212
Arkansas	29
Louisiana	20
New Mexico	34
Oklahoma	50
Texas	79
Overseas - Total	58
Pacific Air Command	
Hawaii	29
Caribbean Area	
Puerto Rico	29

TABLE 46.-- AIRPLANES ON HAND IN AIR NATIONAL GUARD, BY TYPE AND MODEL OF AIRPLANE: MONTHLY, 1948

(Figures are as of end of month)

Type and Model	Jan	Feb	Mar	Apr	May	Jun
Total.............	1,930	1,966	1,998	2,002	2,043	2,034
Continental US – Total........	1,904	1,938	1,972	1,974	2,004	1,991
Combat Airplanes – Total.....	1,460	1,490	1,524	1,530	1,560	1,551
Bomber – Total...........	321	341	347	344	351	344
A-26.................	321	341	347	344	351	344
Fighter – Total..........	1,139	1,149	1,177	1,186	1,209	1,207
P-47.................	419	417	446	455	476	473
P-51.................	720	732	731	731	728	724
P-80.................	-	-	-	-	5	10
Transport – Total..........	111	115	116	116	116	115
C-47.................	109	113	114	114	114	113
C-45.................	2	2	2	2	2	2
Trainer – Total...........	267	267	265	263	263	262
AT-11................	37	37	37	37	37	37
AT-6.................	230	230	228	226	226	225
Communication – Total.......	66	66	67	65	65	63
L-5..................	64	64	65	63	62	61
L-16.................	-	-	-	-	1	-
L-17.................	2	2	2	2	2	2
Overseas – Total............	26	28	26	28	39	43
Combat Airplanes – Total.....	17	17	17	18	30	34
Bomber – Total...........	4	4	4	4	4	4
A-26.................	4	4	4	4	4	4
Fighter – Total...........	13	13	13	14	26	30
P-47.................	13	13	13	14	26	30
Transport – Total..........	3	3	3	3	2	2
C-46.................	3	3	3	3	2	2
Trainer – Total...........	4	6	4	5	5	5
AT-6.................	4	6	4	5	5	5
Communications – Total......	2	2	2	2	2	2
L-5..................	2	2	2	2	2	2

TABLE 46.— AIRPLANES ON HAND IN AIR NATIONAL GUARD, BY TYPE AND MODEL OF AIRPLANE: MONTHLY, 1948
Continued

(Figures are as of end of month)

Type and Model	Jul	Aug	Sep	Oct	Nov	Dec
Total	2,048	2,045	2,029	2,047	2,069	2,148
Continental U. S. - Total	1,998	1,988	1,975	1,991	2,013	2,090
Combat Airplane - Total	1,406	1,396	1,386	1,405	1,428	1,501
Bomber - Total	288	285	280	278	274	271
B-26	288	285	280	278	274	271
Fighter - Total	1,118	1,111	1,106	1,127	1,154	1,230
F-47	458	446	445	445	444	439
F-51	643	638	632	640	644	702
P-80	17	27	29	42	66	89
Transport - Total	115	118	117	116	116	116
C-47/53	113	116	115	114	114	114
C-45	2	2	2	2	2	2
Trainer - Total	416	418	417	417	416	420
T-11	37	36	35	35	35	35
T-6	226	226	225	225	224	225
TB-26	56	58	61	63	66	69
TF-47	18	18	17	15	15	15
TF-51	79	80	79	79	76	76
Communication - Total	61	56	55	53	53	53
L-5	59	54	53	51	51	51
L-17	2	2	2	2	2	2
Overseas - Total	50	57	54	56	56	58
Combat Airplane - Total	39	44	40	41	41	43
Bomber - Total	4	2	1	1	1	1
B-26	4	2	1	1	1	1
Fighter - Total	35	42	39	40	40	42
F-47	35	42	39	40	40	42
Transport - Total	2	2	2	3	3	3
C-46	2	2	2	2	2	2
C-47	-	-	-	1	1	1
Trainer - Total	7	9	10	10	10	10
T-6	7	7	7	7	7	7
TB-26	-	2	3	3	3	3
Communication - Total	2	2	2	2	2	2
L-5	2	2	2	2	2	2

847201 O - 49 - 8

TABLE 47 -- SUMMARY OF AIR NATIONAL GUARD AIRCRAFT ACTIVITIES-DURING 1948

Month	Flying Active Aircraft				Average Number of Pilots	Accident Rate Per 100,000 Hours	Fuel Con-sumption	Total Hours Flown
	Hours Flown	Average Aircraft On Hand	Percent of A/C In Commission	Average Hours Flown Per A/C On Hand				
Jan	9,456	1,597	50	6	2,256	99	643,816	9,459
Feb	12,879	1,726	54	7	2,294	76	956,554	12,892
Mar	17,860	1,800	59	10	2,363	78	1,323,928	17,860
Apr	24,141	1,828	62	13	2,459	66	1,937,965	24,204
May	26,157	1,811	63	14	2,516	56	2,120,557	26,196
Jun	33,508	1,849	65	18	2,583	63	2,362,824	33,538
Jul	24,788	1,837	60	13	2,644	52	1,922,097	24,801
Aug	42,595	1,904	63	22	2,673	91	3,467,714	42,668
Sep	25,991	1,891	60	14	2,722	65	2,213,128	26,058
Oct	22,206	1,897	60	12	2,791	31	1,945,999	22,276
Nov	18,526	1,917	62	10	2,874	86	1,718,411	18,582
Dec	18,586	1,976	60	9	2,989	86	1,617,406	18,638

MILITARY PERSONNEL

Enlistments and Re-enlistments are the only subjects on Military Personnel presented in Vol. II of the 1948 USAF Statistical Digest. These tables continue the information published in the 1947 edition under table number 4C - page 59.

Data has been expanded in the various tables to show more detailed breaks on enlistments, not only Negro and Other than Negro, and Enlistments by Term, but also to show Sex and Grade of Personnel, Women of the Air Force (WAF), and Army with the Air Force (ARWAF).

Enlistments and Re-enlistments are authorized in the Regular Air Force for 3, 4, or 6 years, at the option of the individual enlisting. Re-enlistments are made only in Regular Air Force unassigned.

Immediate Re-enlistments, as shown in some of the tables, are those made the day following discharge from a previous term of service. Re-enlistments made after ninety days, following discharge, are known as re-enlistees with prior service.

Tables 48 and 49 include Aviation Cadets and they are broken out in Table 49. Aviation Cadets must enlist for a period of three years.

Indefinite Enlistments as shown in Tables 49, 51 and 54 were provided for in the Act of 28 June 1947 (Public Law 128 - 80th Congress; sec. VII, Bul 13, WD, 1947) which provided that persons of the first three enlisted grades may be re-enlisted for unspecified periods of time on a career basis. Anyone who serves three or more years of an enlistment for an unspecified period of time may submit his resignation and shall be discharged from his enlistment within 3 months of the submission of such resignation.

The WAF program, as summarized in Tables 51 and 52, was introduced in 1948 by the passage of Bill No. S 1641 by the 80th Congress therefore WAF are reported only from July on through the remainder of the year.

One year enlistments (See AFR, 35-9, 8 Dec'48) were authorized by the Selective Service Act of 1948 (Public Law 759-80th Congress JAAF Bul. 22, 1948), therefore, one year enlistments are reported only for July through December 1948 (See Table 53). One year enlistees are male personnel and exclude Aviation Cadets (as stated above, Aviation Cadets must enlist for the longer period of time). No provision is made for one year enlistments of WAF.

Grades of enlistments as reported in the various tables are defined thus:

First	-	Master Sergeant
Second	-	Technical Sergeant
Third	-	Staff Sergeant
Fourth	-	Sergeant
Fifth	-	Corporal
Sixth	-	Private First Class
Seventh	-	Private

A more complete coverage of Military Personnel statistics may be found in Vol. I of the 1948 USAF Statistical Digest.

88

TABLE 48.-- ENLISTMENTS FOR THE USAF, BY STATUS AS TO PRIOR SERVICE, BY SEX, BY MONTH: JAN THROUGH DEC. 1948.

Note:-- Figures in the table below include Aviation Cadets and Negro personnel; the latter category is broken out in other tables that follow as indicated.

Month	Total Enlist-ments	Status of Previous Service							
		Total Enlistments		No Prior Service		Prior Service		Immediate Re-enlistments	
		Male	Female (WAF)	Male	Female (WAF)	Male	Female (WAF)	Male	Female (WAF)
Total a/	141,176	140,003	1,173	79,482	270	39,327	305	21,194	598
January	14,573	14,573	-	9,413	-	5,005	-	155	-
February	13,362	13,362	-	7,227	-	5,910	-	225	-
March	7,582	7,582	-	3,948	-	3,383	-	251	-
April	8,878	8,878	-	5,475	-	3,232	-	171	-
May	6,455	6,455	-	3,674	-	2,554	-	227	-
June	9,833	9,833	-	7,440	-	2,169	-	224	-
July	9,824	9,812	12	7,553	1	2,024	7	235	4
August	11,819	11,630	189	8,999	1	2,320	47	311	141
September	11,367	10,961	406	7,118	3	2,381	72	1,462	331
October	15,311	15,018	293	6,570	81	3,113	101	5,335	111
November	17,543	17,368	175	6,381	103	3,725	63	7,262	9
December	14,629	14,531	98	5,684	81	3,511	15	5,336	2

a/ Does not include 727 re-enlistments in the Army for AFWAF duty; neither does this figure include 4,289 1 year Air Force enlistees shown in break by term of enlistment. Break for the latter by month may be found under Tables 49 and 53

TABLE 49.-- ENLISTMENTS FOR USAF, BY TERM OF ENLISTMENT, BY SEX, BY MONTH: JAN THROUGH DEC, 1948.

Note:-- Figures in the tables below include Aviation Cadets and Negro personnel; the latter category is broken out in other tables that follow as indicated.

Month	Total	Total		1 Year		2 Year		3 Year		4 Year		5 Year		6 Year		Indefinite	
		Male	Fe-Male (WAF)	Male	Fe-Male (WAF)	Male	Fe-Male (WAF)	Male	Fe-Male (WAF)	Male	Fe-Male (WAF)	Male	Fe-Male (WAF)	Male	Fe-Male (WAF)	Male	Fe-Male (WAF)
Total	145,465	144,292	1,173	4,289	-	-	-	135,358	1,098	525	3	1,975	4	1,970	65	1,075	3
Jan	14,573	14,573	-	-	-	-	-	13,940	-	75	-	558	-	-	-	-	-
Feb	13,362	13,362	-	-	-	-	-	12,689	-	85	-	566	-	2	-	-	-
Mar	7,582	7,582	-	-	-	-	-	7,153	-	38	-	366	-	25	-	-	-
Apr	8,878	8,878	-	-	-	-	-	8,496	-	60	-	145	-	177	-	-	-
May	6,455	6,455	-	-	-	-	-	6,185	-	40	-	63	-	167	-	-	-
Jun	9,833	9,833	-	-	-	-	-	9,699	-	29	-	25	-	80	-	-	-
Jul	10,596	10,584	12	772	-	-	-	9,702	12	25	-	20	-	65	-	-	-
Aug	12,518	12,329	189	699	-	-	-	11,558	179	11	1	14	1	47	8	-	-
Sep	12,371	11,965	406	1,004	-	-	-	10,823	357	22	-	21	2	93	47	2	-
Oct	15,964	15,671	293	653	-	-	-	14,584	285	38	-	59	1	133	6	204	1
Nov	18,153	17,978	175	610	-	-	-	16,614	169	55	-	73	-	154	4	472	2
Dec	15,180	15,082	98	551	-	-	-	13,915	96	47	2	45	-	127	-	397	-

TABLE 50.-- ENLISTMENTS FOR USAF, BY GRADE, BY RACE, BY MONTH: JAN THROUGH DEC, 1948.

(Table below includes 1,173 NAFS but does not include 4,289 one year enlistments and 727 re-enlistments in the Army for AF&AF duty.)

Month	Total Enlistments	First Grade	Second Grade	Third Grade	Fourth Grade	Fifth Grade	Sixth Grade	Seventh Grade	Aviation Cadets
Total	141,176	8,496	8,798	14,782	9,163	7,815	12,225	78,248	1,647
January a/	14,573	62	346	917	1,090	1,468	2,179	8,511	-
February a/	13,362	62	341	980	1,186	1,401	2,264	7,128	-
March	7,582	63	334	766	831	799	1,174	3,606	9
Other Than Negro	7,073	61	329	760	802	745	1,048	3,319	9
Negro	509	2	5	6	29	54	126	287	-
April	8,878	59	274	856	530	543	1,001	5,615	-
Other Than Negro	8,644	59	272	849	517	522	960	5,465	-
Negro	234	-	2	7	13	21	41	150	-
May	6,455	82	216	678	514	367	781	3,815	2
Other Than Negro	6,141	81	214	669	504	344	732	3,595	2
Negro	314	1	2	9	10	23	49	220	-
June	9,833	112	249	610	252	347	714	6,835	714
Other Than Negro	9,540	112	246	603	245	330	683	6,609	712
Negro	293	-	3	7	7	17	31	226	2
July	9,824	140	206	570	261	260	570	7,797	20
Other Than Negro	9,621	139	204	560	256	245	543	7,654	20
Negro	203	1	2	10	5	15	27	143	-
August	11,819	236	312	718	428	299	642	9,184	-
Other Than Negro	11,592	234	311	714	407	281	557	9,088	-
Negro	227	2	1	4	21	18	85	96	-
September	11,367	845	724	1,086	599	301	434	7,157	221
Other Than Negro	10,894	836	707	1,051	554	266	400	6,859	221
Negro	473	9	17	35	45	35	34	298	-
October	15,311	2,487	1,951	2,039	875	527	633	6,122	677
Other Than Negro	14,636	2,460	1,927	1,961	799	465	555	5,795	674
Negro	675	27	24	78	76	62	78	327	3
November	17,543	2,569	2,326	3,024	1,325	764	873	6,658	4
Other Than Negro	16,455	2,510	2,289	2,864	1,186	650	777	6,175	4
Negro	1,088	59	37	160	139	114	96	483	-
December	14,629	1,781	1,519	2,538	1,272	739	960	5,820	-
Other Than Negro	13,452	1,741	1,484	2,373	1,086	583	796	5,389	-
Negro	1,177	40	35	165	186	156	164	431	-

a/ Grade data by race are not available for January and February.

TABLE 51.-- WAF ENLISTMENTS FOR THE USAF BY STATUS AS TO PRIOR SERVICE AND BY TERM OF ENLISTMENT:
JUL THROUGH DEC, 1948.

(Negro personnel are inclosed in parentheses and are not included in the open figures.)

Month	Total Enlistments	Status as to Prior Service			Term of Enlistment				
		No Prior Service	Prior Service	Immediate Re-enlistments	3 Year	4 Year	5 Year	6 Year	In-definite
Total	(82) 1,091	(15) 255	(14) 291	(53) 545	(80) 1,018	2	4	(2) 63	3
July	12	1	7	4	12	-	-	-	-
August	(13) 176	1	47	(13) 128	(13) 166	1	1	8	-
September	(33) 373	3	(4) 68	(29) 302	(33) 324	-	2	47	-
October	(15) 278 a/	81	(4) 97	(11) 100	(13) 272	-	1	(2) 4	1
November	(5) 170 b/	103	(5) 58	9	(5) 164	-	-	4	2
December	(16) 82	(15) 66	(1) 14	2	(16) 80	2	-	-	-

a/ Includes 1 (Other than Negro) Indefinite or Career
b/ Includes 2 (Other than Negro) Indefinite or Career

TABLE 52.-- WAF ENLISTMENTS FOR THE USAF, BY STATUS AS TO PRIOR SERVICE, BY GRADE OF ENLISTMENT,
BY RACE, BY MONTH: JUL THROUGH DEC. 1948.

(Negro personnel are inclosed in parentheses and are not included in the open figures.)

Status of Prior Service by Month	Total	Grade of Enlistment						
		First	Second	Third	Fourth	Fifth	Sixth	Seventh
Total (July through Dec)	(82) 1,091	(2) 22	46	(10) 264	(25) 350	(15) 116	(15) 33	(15) 260
July - Total	12	-	1	4	5	1	-	1
No prior service	1	-	-	-	-	-	-	1
Prior service	7	-	1	4	2	-	-	-
Immediate Reenlistments	4	-	-	-	3	1	-	-
August - Total	(13) 176	(1) 8	11	(1) 55	(6) 85	(2) 15	(3) 2	-
No prior service	10	2	1	3	4	-	-	-
Prior Service	38	1	-	8	24	5	-	-
Immediate Reenlistments	(13) 128	(1) 5	10	(1) 44	(6) 57	(2) 10	(3) 2	-
September - Total	(33) 373	(1) 8	22	(5) 134	(8) 162	(8) 37	(11) 4	6
No prior service	3	-	-	-	1	-	-	2
Prior service	(4) 68	2	4	24	(1) 23	(1) 8	(2) 3	4
Immediate Reenlistments	(29) 302	(1) 6	18	(5) 109	(7) 139	(7) 29	(9) 1	-
October - Total	(15) 278	5	8	(2) 51	(8) 74	(4) 42	(1) 14	84
No prior service	81	-	-	-	-	-	-	81
Prior Service	(4) 97	2	1	16	(2) 30	(2) 32	13	3
Immediate Reenlistments	(11) 100	3	7	(2) 35	(6) 44	(2) 10	(1) 1	-
November - Total	(5) 170	1	2	(2) 17	(2) 21	(1) 17	10	103
No prior service	103	-	-	-	-	-	1	102
Prior Service	(5) 58	1	2	(2) 14	(2) 16	(1) 16	9	-
Immediate Reenlistments	9	-	-	3	5	1	-	-
December - Total	(16) 82	-	2	3	(1) 3	4	3	(15) 67
No prior service	(15) 66	-	-	-	-	-	-	(15) 66
Prior service	(1) 14	-	1	2	(1) 3	4	3	(-) 1
Immediate Reenlistments	(-) 2	-	1	1	(-) -	-	-	(-) -

TABLE 53.-- ONE YEAR ENLISTMENTS FOR USAF, BY STATUS AS TO PRIOR SERVICE, BY RACE, BY MONTH: JUL THROUGH DEC, 1948.

Note:- This table reflects male personnel only as no provision has been made for one year enlistment of WAF. The tables does not include Aviation Cadets. All personnel were enlisted in the Seventh Grade with the exception of 1 man who was enlisted in the Sixth Grade in October.

Month of Enlistment	Status as to Prior Service		
	Total Enlistments	No Prior Service	Prior Service
Total	4,289	4,197	92
July	772	747	25
Other than Negro	699	676	23
Negro	73	71	2
August	699	676	23
Other than Negro	683	660	23
Negro	16	16	-
September	1,004	980	24
Other than Negro	995	971	24
Negro	9	9	-
October	653	648	5
Other than Negro	636	631	5
Negro	17	17	-
November	610	598	12
Other than Negro	597	587	10
Negro	13	11	2
December	551	548	3
Other than Negro	532	529	3
Negro	19	19	-

TABLE 54.-- RE-ENLISTMENTS (OTHER THAN NEGRO AND NEGRO) IN THE ARMY FOR ARWAF DUTY, BY SEX, BY MONTH: APR THROUGH DEC, 1948

(Negro personnel are shown in parentheses and are not included in the open figures)

By Month By Sex	Total	Status as to Prior Service			By Term of Enlistment						
		No Prior Service	Prior Service	Immediate Reenlistment	2 Year	3 Year	4 Year	5 Year	6 Year	In-definite
Total	(124) 603	-	-	(124) 603	9	(118) 551	(1) 2	(4) 5	(1) 6	30
April-Total a/	(3) 4	-	-	(3) 4	-	(2) 3	-	(1) 1	-	-
Male	(3) 4	-	-	(3) 4	-	(2) 3	-	(1) 1	-	-
May-Total	4	-	-	4	-	3	-	1	-	-
Male	4	-	-	4	-	3	-	1	-	-
June-Total	4	-	-	4	-	3	-	1	-	-
Male	4	-	-	4	-	3	-	1	-	-
July-Total	(1) 19	-	-	(1) 19	-	(1) 19	-	-	-	-
Male	(1) 19	-	-	(1) 19	-	(1) 19	-	-	-	-
Female	-	-	-	-	-	-	-	-	-	-
August-Total	(2) 57	-	-	(2) 57	3	(2) 53	-	1	-	-
Male	25	-	-	25	3	22	-	-	-	-
Female	(3) 32	-	-	(3) 32	-	(3) 31	-	1	-	-
September-Total	(14) 77	-	-	(14) 77	4	(14) 70	1	-	2	-
Male	(2) 50	-	-	(2) 50	-	(2) 48	1	-	1	-
Female	(12) 27	-	-	(12) 27	4	(12) 22	-	-	1	-
October-Total	(20) 115	-	-	(20) 115	-	(18) 113	(1) -	(1) -	1	1
Male	(17) 114b/	-	-	(17) 114b/	-	(15) 112	(1) -	(1) -	1	1
Female	(3) 1	-	-	(3) 1	-	(3) 1	(-) -	-	-	-
November-Total	(39) 184c/	-	-	(39) 184	2	(38) 162	1	(1) -	2	17
Male	(39) 182	-	-	(39) 182c/	1	(38) 162	1	(1) -	1	17
Female	(-) 2	-	-	(-) 2	1	(-) -	-	-	1	-
December-Total	(44) 139d/	-	-	(44) 139	-	(42) 125	-	(1) 1	(1) 1	13
Male	(44) 138	-	-	(44) 138d/	-	(42) 124	-	(1) 1	(1) 1	12
Female	(-) 1	-	-	(-) 1	-	(-) 1	-	-	-	-

a/ Initial report.
b/ Includes 1 (Other than Negro) Indefinite or Career
c/ Includes 17 (Other than Negro) Indefinite or Career
d/ Includes 12 (Other than Negro) Indefinite or Career

TABLE 55.-- IMMEDIATE RE-ENLISTMENTS (NEGRO AND OTHER THAN NEGRO) IN THE ARMY FOR ARWAF DUTY, BY SEX, BY GRADE, BY MONTH: APR THROUGH DEC 1948.

(Negro personnel are shown in parentheses and are not included in the open figures.)

By Month By Sex	By Grade of Enlistment														
	Total		First		Second		Third		Fourth		Fifth		Sixth		Seventh	
Total	(124)	603	(5)	119	(11)	99	(21)	150	(22)	121	(40)	69	(20)	30	(5)	15
April a/	(3)	4	-		-		-		(1)	1		2	(2)	1	-	
Male	(3)	4	-		-		-		(1)	1		2	(2)	1		
May	(-)	4	-		-		3			1		-		-	-	
Male	(-)	4	-		-		3			1		-		-	-	
June	(-)	4	-		-		3			-		-		1	-	
Male	(-)	4	-		-		3			-		-		1	-	
July	(1)	19		2		2		4	(1)	4		3		4	-	
Male	(1)	19		2		2		4	(1)	4		3		4	-	
Female		-		-		-		-		-		-		-	-	
August	(3)	57		6		5	(1)	4	(1)	23	(1)	14		3		2
Male	(-)	25		6		3	(-)	2	(-)	9	(-)	2		1		2
Female	(3)	32		-		2	(1)	2	(1)	14	(1)	12		2		-
September	(14)	77		17	(1)	5	(2)	14	(1)	22	(7)	13	(3)	5		1
Male	(2)	50		16	(-)	4		10	(-)	7	(1)	8	(1)	4		1
Female	(12)	27		1	(1)	1	(2)	4	(1)	15	(6)	5	(2)	1		-
October	(20)	115	(2)	35	(1)	26	(4)	24	(3)	12	(10)	9		3		6
Male	(17)	114	(2)	35	(1)	26	(4)	23	(2)	12	(8)	9		3		6
Female	(3)	1	(-)	-	(-)	-	(-)	1	(1)	-	(2)	-		-		-
November	(39)	184	(1)	43	(7)	36	(5)	55	(7)	25	(9)	12	(7)	8	(3)	5
Male	(39)	182	(1)	43	(7)	36	(5)	54	(7)	24	(9)	12	(7)	8	(3)	5
Female	(-)	2	(-)	-	(-)	-	(-)	1	(-)	1	(-)	-	(-)	-	(-)	-
December	(44)	139	(2)	16	(2)	25	(9)	43	(8)	33	(13)	16	(8)	5	(2)	1
Male	(44)	138	(2)	16	(2)	25	(9)	42	(8)	33	(13)	16	(8)	5	(2)	1
Female	(-)	1	(-)	-	(-)	-	(-)	1	(-)	-	(-)	-	(-)	-	(-)	-

a/ Initial report

INDEX

	PAGE
Acceptances, Factory - Airplanes	
All Military	16;17
By plant, by type and model	16;17
by type	15
Airframe weight	18
Definition (See Glossary)	VIII
Navy Cognizance	16;17
USAF Cognizance	16;17
Airframe weight	15
Accidents, Aircraft (See Aircraft Accidents)	74;75
Administrative Flying	64-69
Definition (See Glossary)	VIII
Aircraft Accidents	
Accountable Inventory USAF - Gains and Losses	40-43
By type of accident	74;75
By aircraft and model	74;75
Flying Hours of Aircraft	74;75
Number and Rate	74;75
Aircraft Engines (See Deliveries - engines)	19
Aircraft Production (See Acceptances - Factory)	15-18
Aircraft (See also Airplanes)	
Accidents	74;75
By type and model, Quarterly	74;75
Number and Rate	74;75
Class Designation	11
Flying Time	50A-61
ATC - by type and model	60
Continental US	56;57
By type and model	56;57
MATS - by type and model	61
Overseas	58;59
By type and model	58;59
Summary	50-55
by basic type and model - Monthly	54-55
by Command, by type and model	50-53
On Hand	20-32;34-43;46;48
Continental US, by Command	20;21
by type and principal model	36-37
In Storage at AMC Installations	48
In the USAF, by Type and principal model, monthly	34;35
Overseas	20;21
By type and principal model	38;39
Reserve Forces	20;21
USAF Accountable Inventory, Gains and Losses	40-43
Value of Aircraft parts-Inventory and On-order - Monthly	46
Summary, by Command, by type and model - Quarterly	22-32
Aviation Fuel Consumption	70-73
by Command	70-71
by Type and Model	72-73
Utilization and Maintenance	62-64;69
Aircraft Wrecked - by type and model of aircraft	74-75
Definition (See Glossary)	VIII
Air Defense Command	
Aircraft on Hand - Monthly	20;21
Aviation Fuel Consumption - Monthly	70;71
Flying Time, by type and model of Aircraft	50-52
Utilization and Maintenance of Aircraft	62;63
Summary of Aircraft on Hand, for the USAF, by command, by type and Model, Quarterly	22;24;26;27;29;30

	PAGE
Air Force Reserve	
Aircraft on Hand - Monthly	20;21
Airplanes on Hand, By AF Area	78
By type and model	78
Summary of Air Reserve Activities	80
Summary of Aircraft on Hand for the USAF, by Command, by type and model, Quarterly	23;25;28;31;32
Airframe Weight	
Definition (See Glossary)	VIII
Factory accepted USAF cognizance airplanes	15
By type - Monthly	15
Factory accepted US Military airplanes	16-17
By type - Monthly	16-17
Air Materiel Command	
Aircraft in Storage	48
Aircraft on Hand - Monthly	20-21
Aviation Fuel Consumption - Monthly	70;71
Flying Time, by Type and Model of Aircraft	50-52
Utilization and Maintenance of Aircraft	62-63
Summary of Aircraft on Hand for the USAF, by Command, by Type and Model, Quarterly	22;24;26;27;29;30
Air National Guard	
Aircraft on Hand - Monthly	20;21
Airplanes on Hand, by AF Area and State or Territory	81
Airplanes on Hand, by type and model	84
Factory Deliveries, by type and by recipient	18
Summary of Activities	86
Summary of Aircraft on Hand for the USAF, by Command, by Type and Model, Quarterly	23;25;28;31;32
Airplane Acceptances (See Acceptances - Factory)	15-18
Airplane Deliveries (See Deliveries)	18
Airplane-First Line (See specific type)	
Definition (See Glossary)	X
Airplane - Second Line (See specific type)	
Definition (See Glossary)	X
Airplanes (See Aircraft)	
Authorized for USAF Procurement	12
Average Unit Cost	13
Factory Acceptances	14;15
All Military	15-18
Airframe weight, by Type	18
By Plant, and by Type and Model	16-17
By Type - Monthly	15
USAF Cognizance	14-15
Airframe weight, by Type	15
By Type and Model	14
Factory Deliveries	18
By Type and By Recipient	18
Losses - Airplanes	41,43;47
Aircraft Continental US	47
Aircraft Overseas	47
Inventory	41;43
On Hand	
Cumulative Age Distribution of the USAF Airplane Inventory	44
In Air National Guard	82-85
By AF Area and State or Territory	82;83
By Type and Model	84;85
In Air Reserve, By AF Area and Type and Model	78;79
In Continental US	36;37
By Type and Principal Model	36;37

INDEX — Continued

	PAGE
Airplanes (See Aircraft) (Continued)	
On Hand (Continued)	
In the USAF	33-35
By Major Type - Monthly	33
By Type and Principal Model - Monthly	34-35
In the USAF Accountable Inventory	40-43
By type and principal model	40-43
Overseas	38;39
By type and principal model	38;39
Airplane Losses - Continental US and Overseas	47
Air Proving Ground Command	
Aircraft on Hand (Worldwide) - Monthly	20;21
Aviation Fuel Consumption - Monthly	70;71
Flying Time, by Type and Model of Aircraft	50-52
Utilization and Maintenance of Aircraft	62;63
Summary of Aircraft on Hand for the USAF, by Command, by type and model, Quarterly	22;24;26;27;29;30
Air Training Command	
Aircraft on Hand (Worldwide) - Monthly	20;21
Aviation Fuel Consumption - Monthly	70;71
Flying Time, by type and model of Aircraft	50-52
Utilization and Maintenance of Aircraft	62;63
Summary of Aircraft on Hand for the USAF, By Command, By Type and Model, Quarterly	22;24;26;27;29;30
Air Transport Command (See MATS)	
Flying Time, by type and model	50
By Type and Model, Monthly	51
Utilization and Maintenance of Aircraft	62
Summary of Aircraft on Hand for the USAF, by Command, by Type and Model, Quarterly	22;24
Air University	
Aircraft on Hand (Worldwide) - Monthly	20;21
Aviation Fuel Consumption - Monthly	70;71
Flying Time, by type and model of Aircraft	550-52
Utilization and Maintenance of Aircraft	62;63
Summary of Aircraft on Hand for the USAF, by Command, by Type and Model, Quarterly	22;24;26;27;29;30
Alaskan Air Command	
Aircraft on Hand - Monthly	20;21
Aviation Fuel Consumption, Monthly	70;71
Flying Time, by type and model of Aircraft	51;53
Tactical Units (Groups and Squadrons)	1-9
Utilization and Maintenance of Aircraft	63
Summary of Aircraft on Hand for the USAF, by Command, by type and model, Quarterly	23;25;28;31;32
Army Advisory Group - China	
Flying Time, By Command	51
Flying Time, By type and model	53
Utilization and Maintenance of Aircraft	62
Army Field Forces	18
Factory Deliveries, Airplanes	18
By type and recipient	18
AMAF Duty, Enlistments for	92;93
Aviation Cadet Enlistments	90
Bomber Airplanes	
Aircraft Accidents	74;75
Authorized for USAF Procurement	12
Average Unit Cost	13
Aviation Fuel Consumption	72;73
Cumulative Age Distribution	44

	PAGE
Bomber Airplanes (Continued)	
Factory Acceptances	14-18
All Military	15-17
Airframe Weight	18
Navy Cognizance	16-17
USAF Cognizance	14
Airframe Weight	15
Factory Deliveries, by Recipient	18
Flying Time, By Command	50-55
ATC	60
Continental US	56;57
MATS	61
Overseas	58;59
Summary	50-55
In Storage at AMC Installations	48
Losses	47
On Hand	33-39
Continental US	36;37
In Air National Guard	84;85
In Air Reserve	78;79
Overseas	38;39
USAF Accountable Inventory	40;41
Utilization and Maintenance	64;67
Summary of Aircraft on Hand for the USAF, by Command, by type and Model, Quarterly	22-32
Caribbean Air Command	
Aircraft on Hand (Worldwide) Monthly	20;21
Aviation Fuel Consumption - Monthly	70;71
Flying Time, by type and model of aircraft	53
Tactical Units (Groups and Squadrons)	6
Utilization and Maintenance of Aircraft	63
Summary of Aircraft on Hand for the USAF, by Command, by type and model, Quarterly	23;25;28;31;32
Chief of Staff	
Aviation Fuel	70;71
Utilization and Maintenance	62
By Command	50
By Type and model	52
China (See Army Advisory Group - China)	
Civil Air Patrol	
Aircraft on Hand (Worldwide) - Monthly	20;21
Summary of Aircraft on Hand for the USAF, by Command, by Type and Model, Quarterly	23;25;28;31;32
Cognizance (See Acceptances, Airplanes)	15-18
Definition (See Glossary)	12
Communications Airplanes	
Aircraft Accidents	74-75
Authorized for USAF Procurement	12
Average Unit Cost	13
Aviation Fuel Consumption	72;73
Factory Acceptances	14-18
All Military	15-17
Airframe Weight	18
Navy Cognizance	16-17
USAF Cognizance	14
Airframe Weight	15
Factory Acceptance by Recipient	18
Flying Time, By Command	50-55
ATC	60
Contl US	56;57
MATS	61
Overseas	58;59
Summary	50-55
On Hand	33-39
Continental US	36;37
In Air National Guard	84;85
Overseas	38;39
USAF Accountable Inventory	40;41

INDEX — Continued

	PAGE
Communications Airplanes (Continued)	
Utilization and Maintenance	66;69
Summary of Aircraft on Hand for the USAF, by Command, by Type and Model, Quarterly	22-32
Continental Air Command	
Aircraft on Hand – Quarterly	29;30
Aviation Fuel Consumption – Monthly	70;71
Flying Time, by Type and Model of Aircraft	52
Utilization and Maintenance of Aircraft	62
Continental US (See specific Command or Subject)	
Definition (See Glossary)	IX
Cumulative Age Distribution	44
USAF Airplane Inventory	44
Deliveries – Aircraft Engines	19
All Military	19
By Plant	19
By Model, by Unit Horsepower	19
Jet Propelled, by plant, by model, by unit horsepower	19
Deliveries – Airplane	18
All Military	18
By Type and Recipient	18
Definition (See Glossary)	X
Engines, Aircraft	19
Factory Deliveries	19
Jet Propelled, by Plant, Model and Unit Horsepower	19
All Military	19
by plant, model and unit horsepower	19
Enlistments for USAF	89-92
By Grade	90;91
By Sex	89;92
By Term of	89;91
By Status as to Prior Service	89;91;92
Indefinite	89;91
Negro	90;91;92
One Year	92
Aviation Cadet (See headnote)	92
By Grade (See headnote)	92
By Status of Prior Service	92
Other than Negro	90;91;92
WAF	91
By Grade	91
Negro	91
Other than Negro	91
By Month	91
By Status as to Prior Service	91
By Term of	91
With No Prior Service	89;91;92
With Prior Service	89;91;92
Factory Acceptances (See Acceptances, airplanes)	15-18
Factory Deliveries (See Deliveries – airplanes)	18
Far East Air Forces	
Aircraft on Hand – Monthly	20-21
Aviation Fuel Consumption – Monthly	70-72
Flying time, by type and model of aircraft	51;53
Tactical Units (Groups and Squadrons)	8
Utilization and Maintenance of Aircraft	63
Summary of Aircraft on Hand for the USAF, by Command, by Type and Model, Quarterly	23;25;28;31;32
Fatal Accidents – by Type and Model	74-75
Definition (See Glossary)	X

	PAGE
Fatalities – by type and model	74-75
Definition (See Glossary)	X
Female Enlistments	89-92
Female Re-enlistments	92;93
Fighter Airplanes	
Aircraft Accidents	74-75
Authorized for USAF Procurement	12
Average Unit Cost	13
Aviation Fuel Consumption	72;73
Cumulative Age Distribution	44
Factory Acceptances	14-18
All Military	15-17
Airframe Weight	18
Navy Cognizance	16;17
USAF Cognizance	14
Airframe Weight	15
Factory Deliveries – By Recipient	18
Flying Time, By Command	50-55
Contl US	56
Overseas	58
Summary	50-53
In Storage at AMC Installations	48
Losses	47
On Hand	33-39
Continental US	36;37
In Air National Guard	84;85
Overseas	38;39
USAF Accountable Inventory	40;41
Utilization and Maintenance	64;67
Summary of Aircraft on Hand for the USAF, by Command, by Type and Model, Quarterly	22-32
Flying Time of Aircraft	
Air Transport Command	60
By Type and Model	60
Continental US	56-57
By Type and Model	56;57
Flying Time of AF Pilots on Inactive Duty	80
Military Air Transport Service	61
By Type and Model	61
Overseas	58;59
By Type and Model	58;59
Summary	54;55
By Basic Type and Model	54;55
By Command	50;51;52;53
By type and model	50;51;52;53
Gliders and Targets	
Aviation Fuel Consumption	72;73
Flying Time	55-59
Continental US	56;57
Overseas	58;59
Type and Model, basic	54;55
In Storage at AMC Installations	48
Utilization and Maintenance	66;69
Summary of Aircraft on Hand for the USAF, by Command, by Type and Model, Quarterly	22-32
Groups by Type, Tactical	2-9
Contl US and Overseas Commands	2-4
Overseas Command	5-9
Headquarters Command	
Aircraft on Hand – Monthly	20;21
Aviation Fuel Consumption – Monthly	70;71
Flying Time	52
By type and Model of Aircraft	52
Utilization and Maintenance of Aircraft	62
Summary of Aircraft on Hand for the USAF, by Command, by Type and Model, Quarterly	22;24;26;27;29;30

INDEX — Continued

	PAGE
Immediate Re-enlistments	90-93
Indefinite Enlistments	89;90
Introduction, Tactical Units	1
Definition (See Glossary)	I
Introduction to Enlistments	87
Joint Brazil - US Commission	51;53;63
Flying Time, By Command	51
Flying Time, By Type and Model	53
Utilization and Maintenance of Aircraft	63
Losses, Airplanes (See Airplane Losses)	47
Major Accidents	74;75
By Type and Model of Aircraft	74;75
Definition (See Glossary)	VIII
Male Enlistments	89-92
Male Re-enlistments	92;93
Military Air Transport Service	
Aircraft on Hand - Monthly	20;21
Aviation Fuel Consumption	70;71
By Type and Model	26;27;29;30
Flying Time	53;61
By Type and Model	53;61
Utilization and Maintenance of Aircraft	63
Summary of Aircraft on Hand for the USAF, by Command, by Type and Model, Quarterly	26;27;29;30
Military Enlistments	89-91
Military Re-enlistments	92;93
Minor Accidents	74-75
By Type and Model of Aircraft	74-75
Minimum Individual Training - Flying	64;69
Definition (See Glossary)	X
Miscellaneous Aircraft - Overseas	23;25;28;31;32
National Guard, Ground	18
Factory Deliveries, Airplanes	18
By Type and by Recipient	18
Navy, US	18
Factory Deliveries, Airplanes	18
By Type and by Recipient	18
Negro Enlistments	90-92
Negro Re-enlistments	92;93
Operational Flying	64-69
Definition (See Glossary)	I
Operation VITTLES	53;63;70;71
Aviation Fuel Consumption - Monthly	70;71
Flying Time	53
By Type and Model of Aircraft	53
Utilization and Maintenance of Aircraft	63
Other, Airplanes	
Aircraft Accidents	74;75
Cumulative Age Distribution	44
In Storage at AMC Installations	48
Losses	47
Utilization and Maintenance	64-68
Other, Overseas	
Aircraft on Hand - Monthly	20-32
Aviation Fuel Consumption - Monthly	70;71
Flying Time	53
By Type and Model of Aircraft	53
Utilization and Maintenance of Aircraft	63
Other Than Negro Enlistments	90-92
Other Than Negro Re-enlistments	92;93

	PAGE
Pacific Air Command	
Aircraft on Hand - Monthly	20;21
Aviation Fuel Consumption - Monthly	70;71
Flying Time	50-53
By Type and Model of Aircraft	50-53
Utilization and Maintenance of Aircraft	63
Summary of Aircraft on Hand for the USAF, by Command, by Type and Model, Quarterly	23;25;28;31;32
Parts Aircraft, Value of - In Inventory	46
On Order - Monthly	46
Patrol Bomber	16;17
Factory Acceptances	16;17
Navy Cognizance	16;17
Petroleum Bulk, Storage Capacity	49
Procurement	12;13
USAF-Airplanes Authorized for	12;13
By Type and Model	12
Average Unit Cost	13
Reconnaissance Airplanes	
Aircraft Accidents	74;75
Authorized for USAF Procurement	12;13
Average Unit Cost	13
Aviation Fuel Consumption	72;73
Cumulative Age Distribution	44
Factory Acceptances	14-18
All Military	15-17
Airframe Weight	18
Navy Cognizance	16;17
USAF Cognizance	14
Airframe Weight	15
Factory Deliveries by Recipient	18
Flying Time, By Command	50-55
Continental US	56;57
Overseas	58;59
Worldwide	50-55
In Storage at AMC Installations	48
On Hand	33-39
Continental US	36;37
Overseas	38;39
USAF Accountable Inventory	40;41
Utilization and Maintenance	65;68
Summary of Aircraft on Hand for the USAF, by Command, by Type and Model, Quarterly	22-32
Re-enlistments	89;91-93
By Grade	93
By Sex	92;93
Immediate	89-91;93
In Army for ARNAF	92;93
By Grade	93
By Status of Prior Service	92
By Term	92
Female	92;93
Male	92;93
Negro	92;93
Other than Negro	92;93
Negro	92;93
Other than Negro	92;93
WAF	91
By Grade	91
By Race	91
By Term	91
Research and Development Flying	64-69
Definition (See Glossary)	X
Reserve Forces (See Air Force Reserve)	
Search and Rescue - Aircraft	
Authorized for USAF Procurement	12
Average Unit Cost	13
Aviation Fuel Consumption	72;73

INDEX — Continued

	PAGE
Search and Rescue - Aircraft (Continued)	
Flying Time	50-61
ATC	60
Contl US	56;57
MATS	61
Overseas	58;59
Summary	50-55
On Hand	33-39
Continental US	36;37
Overseas	38;39
USAF Accountable Inventory	42;43
Summary of Aircraft on Hand for the USAF, by Command, by Type and Model, Quarterly	22-32
Separate Squadrons	2-8
By Overseas Commands	5-9
By Type	2-8
Contl US and Overseas	2-4
Special Research Aircraft	
Factory Acceptances	14-18
All Military	15-17
Airframe Weight	18
USAF Cognizance	14
Airframe Weight	15
Factory Deliveries, by Recipient	18
On Hand	33-39
Continental US	36;37
USAF Accountable Inventory	40;41
Squadrons by Type, Separate	2-8
Strategic Air Command	
Aircraft on Hand - Monthly	20-21
Aviation Fuel Consumption - Monthly	70;71
Flying Time	50;53
Utilization and Maintenance of Aircraft	62;63
Summary of Aircraft on Hand for the USAF, by Command, by Type and Model, Quarterly	22;24;26;27;29;30
Tactical Air Command	
Aircraft on Hand (Worldwide) - Monthly	20;21
Aviation Fuel Consumption - Monthly	70;71
Flying Time	50-52
By Type and Model of Aircraft	50-52
Utilization and Maintenance of Aircraft	63
Summary of Aircraft on Hand for the USAF, by Command, by Type and Model, Quarterly	22;24;26;27;29;30
Tactical Groups and Separate Squadrons (Contl US and Overseas)	
By Overseas Command	5-9
Alaska	7
Caribbean Air Command	6
FEAF	8
PAC	9
Europe	
Definition (See Glossary)	x
Continental US	2-4
Continental US and Overseas Summary	2-4
Introduction	1
Overseas	2-4
Targets and Gliders (See Gliders and Targets)	
Trainer - Airplanes	
Aircraft Accidents	74-75
Authorized for USAF Procurement	12-13
Average Unit Cost	13
Aviation Fuel Consumption	72;73
Cumulative Age Distribution	44
Factory Acceptances	14-18
All Military	15-17
Airframe Weight	18
Navy Cognizance	16-17
USAF Cognizance	14
Airframe Weight	15

	PAGE
Trainer - Airplanes (Continued)	
Factory Deliveries by Recipient	18
Flying Time, By Command	50-55
ATC	60
Continental US	56;57
MATS	61
Overseas	58;59
Summary	550-55
In Storage at AMC Installations	48
On Hand	33-39
Continental US	36;37
In Air National Guard	84;85
In Air Reserve	78
Overseas	38;39
USAF Accountable Inventory	40;41
Utilization and Maintenance	64;67
Transport and Cargo Airplanes	
Aircraft Accidents	74;75
Authorized for USAF Procurement	12;13
Average Unit Cost	13
Aviation Fuel Consumption	72;73
Cumulative Age Distribution	44
Factory Acceptances	14-18
All Military	15-17
Airframe Weight	18
Navy Cognizance	16;17
USAF Cognizance	14
Airframe Weight	15
Factory Deliveries by Recipient	18
Flying Time, By Command	50-55
ATC	60
Contl US	56;57
MATS	61
Overseas	58;59
Summary	50-55
In Storage at AMC Installations	48
On Hand	33-39
Contl US	36;37
In Air National Guard	84;85
In Air Reserve	79
Overseas	38;39
USAF Accountable Inventory	40;41
Utilization and Maintenance	65;68
Units in Continental US and Overseas, Tactical	1-9
US Air Forces in Europe	
Aircraft on Hand - Monthly	20;21
Aviation Fuel Consumption - Monthly	70;71
Flying Time, by Type and Model of Aircraft	50-53
Tactical Units (Groups and Squadrons)	5
Utilization and Maintenance of Aircraft	63
Summary of Aircraft on Hand for the USAF, by Command, by Type and Model, Quarterly	23;25;28;31;32
Vittles, Operation	53;63;70;71
WAF Enlistments	90;91
By Grade	91
By Month	90;91
By Race	90;91
By Status of Previous Service	90;91
By Term of Enlistment	90

U.S. GOVERNMENT PRINTING OFFICE : O—1949

Printed in Great Britain
by Amazon